W9-BLO-834

Praise for *TELL THE TRUTH*

"Truth is a tricky issue to discuss, but Unerman and Baskin do a great job in explaining how to be truthful and yet create effective advertising messages." —AL RIES,
Coauthor, *War in the Boardroom*

"Truth is the only defensible competitive advantage. I'm not sure why this is controversial, but it's true." —SETH GODIN,
Author, *We Are All Weird*

"The true future of marketing will be about brands and their ability to have a direct relationship with their consumers. The trick, as so well explained in *Tell The Truth*, is that brands have to be honest . . . brutally honest. Truth in advertising? Truth in marketing? It hasn't really happened, but now it can. Sue Unerman and Jonathan Salem Baskin offer this wonderful book as a first step in the right direction. It belongs on everyone's desk who touches a brand." —MITCH JOEL,
President of Twist Image and blogger, podcaster, and author, *Six Pixels of Separation*

"Truth in advertising is no longer an oxymoron; it's an absolute necessity if a brand wishes to compete in today's increasingly transparent marketplace. Brands will be judged not based on what they say, but what they do; not the promises they make, but the ones they keep. This book is the first step toward your enlightenment." —JOSEPH JAFFE, Author, *Flip the Funnel*

"The authors re-examine the abiding value of authenticity; convince us that, in the Internet age, brand truth has become a marketing necessity; and offer practical guidance on how to achieve it." —SIR MARTIN SORRELL,
CEO, WPP

"*Tell the Truth* is an essential guide to advertising in the modern world." —JONATHAN DEAN,
Online Culture Editor, *The Sunday Times*

"In a sea of marketing gibberish and thinly disguised motivational babble designed less to boost sales than to funnel cash from the confused into consultants' pockets, Unerman and Baskin stand out by offering practical information presented in plain English." —KEN WHEATON,
Managing Editor, *Advertising Age*, and author,
The First Annual Grand Prairie Rabbit Festival

"In the digital age, all of us have a voice that can be heard instantly and around the world. Consumers are increasingly using that voice to speak out whenever they see injustice and untruth. So for brands and businesses, honesty and integrity are now imperative for success. *Tell the Truth* is an essential guide to building honest businesses." —CLAIRE BEALE,
Editor, *Campaign*

Tell the
TRUTH

AUTHENTIC

Tell the TRUTH

AUTHENTIC

Honesty
Is Your
Most
Powerful
Marketing
Tool

Sue Unerman and
Jonathan Salem Baskin

BenBella Books, Inc. | Dallas, Texas

Copyright © 2012 by Sue Unerman and Jonathan Salem Baskin

All rights reserved. No part of this book may be used or reproduced in any manner whatsoever without written permission except in the case of brief quotations embodied in critical articles or reviews.

BenBella

BenBella Books, Inc.
10300 N. Central Expressway, Suite 400
Dallas, TX 75231
www.benbellabooks.com
Send feedback to feedback@benbellabooks.com

Printed in the United States of America

10 9 8 7 6 5 4 3 2 1

Library of Congress Cataloging-in-Publication Data is available for this title.
978-1-936661-46-6

Editing by Debbie Harmsen
Copyediting by Lisa Miller
Proofreading by Michael Fedison
Indexing by Debra Bowman
Cover design by Faceout Studio
Text design and composition by Neuwirth & Associates, Inc.
Printed by Bang Printing

Distributed by Perseus Distribution
(www.perseusdistribution.com)

To place orders through Perseus Distribution:
Tel: (800) 343-4499
Fax: (800) 351-5073
E-mail: orderentry@perseusbooks.com

Significant discounts for bulk sales are available. Please contact Glenn Yeffeth at glenn@benbellabooks.com or (214) 750-3628.

Contents

Introduction

The Case for Truth

Truth in advertising has long been something to ignore or interpret creatively, if not intentionally avoid altogether. The role of advertising has been to show brands in their best possible light, of course, in order to convince consumers that the products being pitched are imbued with stellar qualities. In a word, traditional advertising has often been about a ruse, or hype, if you prefer.

This skewed positioning worked when the brand's voice was the only one speaking to consumers, but with the rise of social media, that era is over. In our current age, a brand's image is not only a result of the carefully crafted brand architecture transmitted by marketers but is also dependent on the conversations and experiences of millions of consumers.

Today, consumers will learn the truth and/or determine what's true, and smart companies have realized that every communications medium can be used to contribute to those conclusions.

But what marketers are telling consumers often isn't jiving with what they're telling each other. So consumers' distrust, disbelief, and disinterest seem to increase with every passing year. Ignoring the truth with propaganda, clouding it in spin, or obscuring it with technologically enabled entertainment might feel good and might even win industry awards, but these once-great traditions of marketing and advertising are dying or are, in fact, already dead. No new technology or creative tactic can keep up the pretenses of marketing—no matter how expertly renewed and delivered—in an age when we are digitally empowered to find out everything we need or want to know.

It's not enough to talk anymore; the way to win is through using all of the means at your disposal to tell the truth. The brands that tell the truth are the ones that are the most successful, while the brands that entertain and spin are the ones that will get found out, whose self-aggrandizing will be exposed.

Truth is a powerful marketing tool and the only way to really promote a message and brand effectively. If your brand is more truthful in the future than it has been in the past, if your brand is more truthful than its competitors, and if it is more truthful than consumers expect, then it will win. It will stand out as a brand of integrity. What you see is what you get. Brands that have a process for telling the truth are likely to sell more products, make more money, and keep more customers loyal—through any medium, in every market.

Brands that have a process for telling the truth are likely to sell more products, make more money, and keep more customers loyal—through any medium, in every market.

Truth is the only sustainable competitive advantage available to brands these days, since there are always ways to improve it, and always the chance that competitors will fail to do so. The journey never ends, but brands can always get quicker, faster, and better at being truthful.

This book is about how you can make your brand and marketing communications more truthful. And it's about why your business needs it now more than ever.

Defining Truth

So what do we mean by truth?

First, let's address what it's *not*. Truth in marketing is not about telling would-be purchasers of an expensive fragrance that most of the purchase price goes into the packaging rather than the ingredients of the perfume. It's not about admitting that a car won't make you cool, or that shopping at a crowded retail store might not be fun. In other words, truth doesn't have to mean full disclosure of every possible fact. It means marketing with honesty.

Now for what truth *is*. Truth in branding, like truth in life, is about authenticity, fair dealing, and simple straight talk. For a brand to be truthful, it must genuinely deliver against its image and elevate that image to become an understanding or judgment that is not just projected by its advertising and marketing, but reflected in the opinions and beliefs of its consumers. Communication about the brand must be clear, believable, and consistent in all its content and across all media channels. We call the sum of this content and context the brand truth.

In this sense, truth is not a new idea, really. Successful and sustainable brands have always delivered great truths, even if they weren't specifically articulated as the brand strategies. For many other brands, telling the truth has been but one choice out of many for a successful strategy, depending on audience and circumstances.

But truth has always been the underlying criteria for brand perceptions and beliefs. For example, even though for decades the tobacco companies' marketing ignored or fought health concerns raised by their products, consumers still perceived the truth, and the brands' reputations suffered accordingly. We've seen it more recently when video claiming rotten baggage service on a major airline emerged on YouTube in 2009; it garnered millions of hits, but the airline's brand was unaffected because consumers believed they already knew whatever truths the video may have communicated. While marketers praised it as proof of the efficacy of social media, the medium was not the story here, since the video contained no new truths that mattered to anyone.

Conversely, think of how Volkswagen (VW) advertised its Beetle in the United States in the late 1950s ("Think Small"), building upon natural perceptions of the car, or when Steve Jobs acknowledged his brand's unavoidable past performance when he introduced Apple's iCloud service in the summer of 2011 by saying: "Now you may think, why should I believe them? They're the ones who brought me MobileMe. Let me just say it wasn't our finest hour, but we learned a lot."

Truth can also mean giving consumers immediate access to facts, whether in cola brands challenging one another to taste tests in the United States in the 1980s, or Direct Line motor insurance brand in the United Kingdom today giving the public a direct line to straightforward and clear pricing, instead of going through intermediaries with undisclosed commissions.

The opposite of brand truth is not a flat-out lie. Lying in advertising or being deceitful in social media campaigns is illegal and will get you prosecuted. The opposite of brand truth is entertainment and spin . . . the *absence* of truth. It's giving up responsibility for enabling consumers to understand the truth about your brand. You only have to turn on the TV or glance at a social media site to see an example of creativity without truthful meaning, or conversation without meaningful content. We believe that this is insanely short-term. It's just too easy to be found out and held accountable. If a brand has an ad that relies on an adorable talking animal, it simply distracts attention from the brand truth and fails to establish or strengthen an understanding with its consumers. It therefore will not sustain any kind of competitive advantage against a brand that uses similar opportunities to speak truthfully. If a brand relies on a pop star's endorsement or Internet video buzz to make up for return on investment (ROI), its brand value will be harder to quantify or link to subsequent purchase behavior, and word-of-mouth will be ephemeral and fleeting (and not necessarily positive).

We have investigated hundreds of case studies in sector after sector only to discover that the best brand truths have sustained success while brand entertainment and brand spin fail to deliver in the long-term. Sometimes an entire sector comes face-to-face with this truth. Many of us grew up with fantastic advertising sagas around instant coffee, a household staple that was fine until coffee shops started selling the real deal on every corner and no amount of image advertising could make you believe instant brands were as sophisticated and delicious as the real thing. The entire travel industry crashed headlong into truth when the Internet threw off the

blinders that had kept consumers from comparing transpor-
tation and destination experiences, allowing them to come
up with their own consensus definitions of what brands meant
(and how much they were worth).

Again, let's be clear: we are not talking about an idea of
absolute truth. Brand truth does not mean disillusioning your
customers about all and any brand attributes. This isn't about
moving from the world of image to the world of utility. Nor is
it about renouncing emotion in favor of reason. It is not another expression of the no-logo movement of the early years
of the twenty-first century. Brands still have huge power.

The question is how can your brand use truth to be more
powerful than your competition? In the chapters that follow,
we'll show you how to ensure your brand truth is better than
the rest. But first, let us explain why we went on this quest for
better marketing and reached these conclusions about truth.

The Case for Truth

Half a century ago, advertising pioneer David Ogilvy said,
"The consumer is not a moron, she's your wife."

Now, the consumer is the expert who knows everything
about your brand. What's missing can be uncovered in thirty
seconds on a smartphone from a variety of sources.

So we set out on this project more than two years ago to test
a different, more fundamental approach to this marketing conundrum: could truth be the quality that distinguishes good
marketing from bad? We combined our more than half-century
of experience at some of the world's largest advertising agencies, at which we've worked for many of the top global brands,
and then went further, studying hundreds of additional brands
and cases, and interviewing dozens of experts.

We discovered that the absence of brand truth is the primary
reason why marketing communications fail or, what's more

common these days, why they can claim tactical success without furthering business strategy. Businesses that don't pursue truth-telling, or assume it's a matter of suggestion or spin, aren't as much exploiting the wrong approach as simply missing the right one. They have connections without substance, enter-tainment without relevance, and content without meaning.

Clarifying the truth, and striving to do so consistently, is what makes the latest marketing tools work better and more efficiently.

We found a far more fundamental answer: brand truth works. It's the understanding that drives sustainable conver-sations, storytelling, and consumer engagement. Clarifying the truth, and striving to do so consistently, is what makes the latest marketing tools work better and more efficiently. It's the oldest new idea under the sun.

The Eight Ways to Deliver Brand Truth

Based on research of hundreds of companies and in-depth case studies on more than fifty global brands to show us how truthful brands deliver sales, profits, and sustainable relation-ships, we uncovered the eight ways brands define and deliver the truth. We've distilled those eight actions into a set of tools that you can apply to your business as you read each chapter. These are the eight actions we've identified as the ones that convey truth to your buyers. Use more of them on your brand and you'll increase your likelihood of success and move your sales and customer loyalty forward.

Part One (the first four chapters) is concerned with what you *can* say and what you *should* say about your brand (i.e., the content of your brand marketing). Consumer experience doesn't lie, so the challenge is to acknowledge that experience, not paint over it or ignore it. Truthful content is additive. Others tell and affirm it, so it's cheaper and easier than any other approach. Internet and mobile search means that it's always there and always growing.

Truths are built up over time, which makes them sticky, and they are far more compelling and resistant to change than any other dynamic. When you have truth as part of your brand, consumers are far more likely to forgive your mistakes in service or delivery than they would otherwise. They don't just believe or like what you've told them. They trust it.

Part Two (the second group of four chapters) is concerned with how you tell the truth. It is a guide to creating context for your communications that will enhance the integrity of your brand. The context can make an immediate difference to the plausibility of the message. How you communicate can show your willingness to accept and respond to feedback—an essential attribute in the era of Twitter and Facebook (and whatever comes next).

The context also allows you to invite consumers to be a part of the brand story. They are able to get involved in completing the image of the brand according to their own experiences.

Here are the eight actions that will deliver better brand truths and correspond to the next eight chapters:

1. **Acknowledge reality.** Take account of your consumers' understanding of reality before you try to change it. Address what the consumers know is true before trying to persuade them of something different. Truth isn't an inconsequential sliver, a spin, or a case you want to make to the world; rather, it's the totality of your consumers' understanding, beliefs, and fears. There are certain techniques

for developing content that recognizes what is going on in the real world and can then be used to shift consumer understanding to a new, more truthful understanding.

2. **Deliver real changes to services and company structure.** The processes your brand engages in are important determinants of how truthful your content will be. Consumers will only believe you if what you tell them is not just what you say but also what you do. You can't win people over these days with just a plausible message; your words must be made tangibly real through your very practices and implementation. There are "internal" and "external" examples of what this means and how some companies have changed what they do so as to affirm truth. We explore both aspects of this with specific examples.

3. **Take the consumer on your brand truth journey with you.** Tell customers clearly what you want them to know and give them a clearly signposted path to discovering it (not just a portion or version of it). Enable your consumers to discover and explore the brand truth for themselves. Truth is a journey for them with your brand, and we have discovered some key ways in which brands have used content to signpost the consumer journey to deliver behavior change. The punch line here? Don't be vague. Meaning, don't communicate a "warm fuzzy" about your brand. Be specific and directional.

4. **Enlist third-party advocates.** Third-party advocates are essential. Third-party involvement—not just as audiences of "influencers" but active *codefiners*—must be an integral part of your brand truth, both to help create it and then to defend it over time. Just like your brand can no longer declare truth in a vacuum, it is no longer enough to declare it alone. Your audiences are no longer passive recipients of your information. There is

a spectrum of participants who contribute to defining truth in this new way and who require different levels of involvement depending on the status and openness of the brand. We explore the roles of each with a specific case and draw conclusions on how they influence brand truth communications.

5. **Be close. Be "close" to home.** However huge or global an idea might be, it is experienced locally. Recognizing this and using this quality to competitive advantage has huge power. Also, exploiting nearness and delivering its true relevance can differentiate between what's believed and what's not. "Nearness" has multiple dimensions, each providing a different avenue to communicating information that is more personal and more personally relevant. We share with you each aspect of being close to home that we examined and the tools we derived that make nearness a core component of brand truth communications.

6. **Find a Truth Turning Point (TTP).** Truth isn't just an extended narrative over time, but a moment—a Truth Turning Point—when brands challenge conventions, defy expectations, and surprise consumers by speaking directly to them. Such TTPs can transform almost any medium into a prompt for behavior or attitude change. If you can find and use them in the right way, they are extremely positive. Conversely, the wrong kind of TTP can work against you. There are very specific ways to create TTPs, and we explore each in detail.

7. **Use point-of-action media.** Few brands fully exploit the context of their messaging by ensuring the content is delivered at the time when it is most useful and therefore easiest to act on or do something about. Communicating with consumers usefully is a great way to deliver brand truths, and we studied extensively the ways that

brands make utility a core component of how and where they deliver their marketing communications.

8. **Leverage routine.** Leverage the power of a new routine. Most people spend most of their time in routine activity. If you can either fit into an established routine or create a new one, then your brand wins. If you can become the routine truth for your customer, then the clutter of everyday living works to your advantage. This chapter shows how several major brands won business advantage by leveraging routines instead of trying to overcome them.

Brand truth exists and it can work for you. It's unavoidable, additive, and very sticky, and its experience is immediate, useful, and ongoing. *Tell the Truth* is your detailed guide for creating and delivering it. We demonstrate how you can make your brand and marketing communications more truthful, and why your business needs it now more than ever.

Please keep in mind that ours is a comprehensive strategy that uses every weapon in your communications arsenal. Brand truth has been a fact for many decades and is not inherent in any medium or channel; in fact, we've found examples of it that span the last fifty years, and present them so you can see beyond the promises and biases of what might be most popular or easiest today. Truth has always been there, ready for brands to embrace and exploit. We want to show you how.

We also believe in practicing what we preach, which is why we've maintained the website and blog "The Brand Truth Project" since early 2011 at www.tellthetruthbook.com.

Thank you to everyone who contributed comments, ideas, or reached out to one of us directly. The simple fact that we started talking about truth was itself a great contributor not only to our thinking but also the efforts of others over the past two years. Again, thanks for your involvement.

We believe that once you start thinking about brand truth, you'll see the world differently in general and our profession in particular. You'll realize that we're surrounded by promises that, at first blush, just can't be true: unhealthy foods that are good for you, energy futures that deny our energy past, and technology devices that will introduce you to a new Garden of Eden. You'll see channels of content filled with empty calories of information, conversations that don't really converse, and the hopes and needs of manufacturers trying desperately to create demand. And you'll see the immense and important opportunity to make these efforts more truthful.

This book is a manifesto backed with dozens of real-world examples. Our premise is simple: truth sells. Brands that are most truthful will be the most successful and those that rely on entertainment or resort to spin instead of truth-telling will ultimately fail. Your brand needs to tell the truth, and the sooner the better.

Use this book as a guide to action. Through the course of the next eight chapters, we will continue to make the case for telling the truth and give you a set of criteria that, when put into practice, can give your brand the competitive advantage that truth-telling provides.

Finally, the conclusions and opinions in *Tell the Truth* are our own and do not reflect those of our employers or clients. While we relied on many of our associates and friends to help us develop our thinking, and many of them are quoted in the pages that follow, any factual or interpretive errors are ours, not theirs. Sue wants to thank everyone who works at MediaCom, and we both thank our clients and colleagues, past and present, without whom much of the great work mentioned here wouldn't have happened. Both of us are blessed by the company we keep and we value it tremendously.

Sue and Jonathan

PART ONE

CONTENT

Although the U.S. Constitution listed three truths that its framers believed were self-evident in the late eighteenth century, successive generations have grappled with differing and sometimes contradictory interpretations of what those truths really meant. "To tell you the truth" and "Honestly . . ." are colloquialisms that are intended to prequalify statements that follow as less deceitful than those said just prior. Truth is often a synonym for an opinion, belief, or narrowly defined slice of information.

For something so simple, truth is complicated. It's why many businesses and institutions avoid addressing it head-on. We think they do so to their own detriment. Your consumers seek truth in everything you share with them, even if they don't always do so explicitly or purposefully. They also know when it's not there; no amount of creativity or conversation, no matter how entertaining or even memorable, can take its place. If you're not contributing to a truthful relationship with your consumers in everything you share with them, you risk being left on the sidelines. They'll come up with the truth about your brand whether or not you like it, agree with it, or had anything to do with it.

We wrote *Tell the Truth* so you would have a guide to taking charge of your role in establishing and sustaining a shared understanding of truth with your consumers. We'll explore how the variables of context contribute to delivering it in the second half of this book. The first half is focused on the content that must populate and inform that context.

To us, "content" isn't simply what you propagate through ads and social media campaigns, it's *why* you do it. It is everything to which your brand is attached. Traditionally, this has not all been under the control or influence of the marketing team. The marketing team will spend significant time and money to hone a brand image, and then this image might be shattered the very first time the consumer interacts with the complaints department—that's if they can get through by phone or by email at all. On the other hand, great content will cement your brand image—content addresses your consumers' understanding of your brand, and not the qualities you hope to attach to it through artifice or engagement. We've looked at hundreds of successful companies that have found ways to deepen their consumer relationships through sharing content that people needed, wanted, and used. Far from being boringly utilitarian, these brands have found innovative ways to address the truth and use it to their competitive advantage.

It is our belief that great marketers in future will have to insist on influencing all the content attached to a brand or the brand will not succeed as it has been able to do in the past, just relying on advertised image alone. We know truth when we see it. A truthful idea sticks with us and makes its source more credible even if we're not thrilled with its substance. Before we look at ways to deliver it, the content of truth deserves some serious exposition.

1

Acknowledge Reality

"**W**ait a minute," 24 Hour Fitness CEO Carl Liebert said at an internal meeting in early 2010. "We don't tell anybody this and then we wonder why they quit?"

He was talking about the worst-kept secret in the fitness business: your results are only as good as your effort, and there's a better than even chance you won't get what you want. Billions are spent annually to help would-be customers avoid this big, *er*, fat point, preferring to sell miracle cookies, wacky machines, diet subscriptions, and other gimmicks intended to let people fool themselves into believing they can buy their way to losing weight and getting in shape. Fitness clubs aren't necessarily included in the same category as secret weight-loss potions, but Liebert and his chief marketer, Tony Wells, were reviewing some troubling focus group information that suggested many new members were not only intimidated by the facilities but often felt they needed to get into shape *before* they even dared show up.

"Our industry has done it to itself," Wells explained. He added:

> Most Americans want to lose a few pounds and feel better about themselves, and there are so many businesses out there offering gimmicks that have little chance of working. It's simple math, really: if you end each day with a five-hundred-calorie deficit below what you regularly consume, you'll lose a pound by the end of the week, and working out can help you get there. There's no way around it, yet dropping somebody into a gym is not really getting them started on that path.

Standard marketing canon would suggest that gyms shouldn't address this fact head-on because consumers don't want to be told the truth, especially on something as difficult as losing weight. That's why the business strategy for most gyms resembles that of car dealerships: sign up new clients—called "customer ups"—and get them to commit to multiyear contracts that have a good chance of never getting used after the first few months of membership. Think extended-service agreements for consumer electronics products that will be obsolete long before the contracts expire. What happens before then is that around 40 percent of gym customers move on to shop for the next trick that might help them accomplish their goals. For 24 Hour Fitness, a third of its new members were referrals from those older members who defied the attrition rate.

The math just didn't add up for anybody, neither the brand nor its customers. "So we decided to acknowledge the reality of exercise head-on," said Wells, "and we oriented everything about our experience to do it."

Wait, a fitness product that doesn't guarantee success with little to no effort? You could hear the shudders through late-night TV infomercials. "No," Wells added. "We just committed to telling our customers how to succeed and then made sure we oriented our offering to support them in their efforts to reach their goals."

The evolution of thinking at 24 Hour Fitness had been under way for years, starting in 2006 when Liebert arrived, with its commitment to improving the fundamentals of its business. Bucking the trend of using social media to chase down problems after they happen, it dove deep into every customer complaint (it managed somewhat of a backlog of them) to discover what needed to change in order to prevent complaints in the future. Clubs were given greater voice in operational decisions and more latitude in resolving issues. Within thirty-six months, the chain went from a failing rating by the Better Business Bureau to an A+, and it was the first (and the only) fitness brand to use J.D. Power and Associates to measure new and existing member satisfaction.

Wells calls marketing "a story well told," and 24 Hour Fitness wanted to get the elements of its plot in place before creating the narrative to promote it. "We wanted to be the brand that consumers could trust, and that meant first deserving their trust. It wasn't a marketing challenge but an operational imperative."

"We wanted to be the brand that consumers could trust, and that meant first deserving their trust. It wasn't a marketing challenge but an operational imperative." — Tony Wells, 24 Hour Fitness

"Truth in Fitness" campaign was launched in late 2010 after six months in development with its advertising agency Barkley, based in Kansas City. Arguably, the content was not particularly creative or funny, and it didn't use a known celebrity spokesperson. The online spots relied on actual club staff talking about the truths of working out: the time commitment, the necessity of that commitment, and reassurance that there's a payoff at the end of that investment—better health and fitness. Club signage echoed these themes.

Current members reacted to the new campaign with compliments and, in some notable instances, relief. In what might be the single most truth-telling innovation, the brand gave up its year-plus membership requirements and now allows members to go month to month. The expectation is that this better links to their actual experience.

"Once we established our game plan and got alignment, we went about being journeymen and getting it done," Wells adds. "Our brand is about telling people the truth and then backing it up with their experience, so we're supporting the campaign with our operations. That's getting us a lot more marketing impact than a campaign focused on some invented benefits would do."

Initial results substantiate the approach. Customer acquisition costs are down, there is double-digit EBITDA (earnings before interest, taxes, depreciation, and amortization) growth, J.D. Power member satisfaction is up, employee engagement is up double digits, and employee turnover has seen a 50 percent improvement. 24 Hour Fitness liked the results so much that in 2011 it took its commissioned sales to non-commissioned. It was the first national fitness chain to do so.

While an overt example of truth-telling—the campaign was called "the truth about fitness," after all—it illustrates a core quality of the content of any truth: it must acknowledge reality. Seems simple, right? It's not, nor is it particularly common. Most brand promises either ignore reality or presume to step above or beyond it. Like Wells told us, the implicit promise that the latest diet or fitness miracle will work avoids explicit mention of the fact that the last ones failed. Hope springs eternal, and most product launches take the same approach, choosing to promote some benefit that somehow transcends the disappointments that constitute much of reality. "More cleaning power" is a common refrain, without ever specifying what constituted "lesser" cleaning capacity. "More taste," "enhanced speed," and "fewer calories" are other pitches that ring less true because they skip defining the truth they're qualifying. It's as if we expect that consumers are lost in some vague, memory-less, and fact-free place. The exact opposite is true. Our pitches are less believable, less effective, and less sustainable.

When we don't acknowledge the truth, we may be lying. As we mentioned in the introduction, David Ogilvy's famous refrain that consumers aren't strangers but rather your wife is rendered anew by our technology and our culture. Now it's more personal: your consumer is you, at least intellectually and morally, so you're not smarter. When you know something is only partially true, he or she does, too.

We wanted to understand how brands approach developing content to tactically acknowledge reality, and we saw five broad ways, which we've named the Five Fs:

1. Forceful
2. Functional
3. Funny
4. Fair
5. Forecasted

24 Hour Fitness showed us the forceful approach: tell people you're telling them the truth and then tell it to them. It's one of the five ways to develop and focus content so that it will be truthful. Now let's move to the next.

Functional: Can Facts Be Sexy?

Automotive dealers tend to dislike the marketing that comes
from manufacturers. It's an eternal tug-of-war, a battle of personalities and perspective, an ethereal yin versus a material
yang. Dealers want commercials and brochures that promote
the functional components of cars and trucks that they find
themselves selling on showroom floors, while manufacturers
want to build the emotional and associative benefits of brands.

Both approaches are right, of course; GM proved the power
of automotive branding when it invented the "good, better,
best" styling strategy for its models in the late 1920s and gave
consumers visually obvious as well as functional differences
upon which to base their purchase preferences. The answer
has always been in finding the right balance. Today, it's just
a lot harder to do. The truths of global sourcing and manufacturing, similarities of design across model types (due in
part to shared platforms and more brands chasing the same
consumers), and shared approaches to ownership and pricing
have made it harder to find that balance (and challenged many
preconceived notions about each approach). We must admit
that we'd be happy never to see another commercial featuring
a car driving way too fast down a deserted highway (it is a stereotype utterly devoid of any truth), or be forced to endure an
excruciatingly overproduced creative spot . . . either of which
could be used to market any vehicle. Both vehicle function
and brand identity approaches have their shortcomings.

Ford has been at the forefront of experimentation. One
angle requires a complete shift to the branding end of the
content spectrum through the effective outsourcing of its
marketing to the public. For instance, its foray into social
media with its "Fiesta Movement" campaign paid twentysome-
thing bloggers to talk about the Fiesta (provided by Ford for
the purpose) and participate in various "missions" that were

featured in videos on YouTube. None of the participants were car people, which was the point. Some of Ford's 2011 advertising for its new Explorer was developed using feedback from tens of thousands of its Facebook fans, also unqualified by anything other than having "friended" the brand online. The company reported that these and other related activities prompted increased pre-leads, online inquiries, and reservations for dealership visits.

Turning such leads into sales could well require the same functional selling that the dealerships would normally want to see in the outbound marketing (though we're sure they didn't complain about the foot traffic), so exploring this angle didn't change the dynamic balance between the two approaches as much as avoid it altogether. It certainly helped that both vehicles were among the best in their class technically, priced to sell, and looked damn good.

We're fascinated by another angle, evidenced by Ford's F-150 campaign that began in 2008. Dubbed the "rant," the spots were based on functional attributes read with considerable attitudinal swagger by actor Dennis Leary in syncopation with large-type print on the screen. It was a gutsy move, hatched with agency WWP in a pre-crash economy that could have easily encouraged the Ford brand marketers to embrace the winding roads and celebrity nonsense that flush budgets tend to attract. The rant spots were still creative—Leary's tone and even the pacing of his speaking voice add associative qualities to the brand—but the core was functional ... functional, factual, truthful. The F-150 is within a vehicle category that tends toward RPMs and hauling capacity, but consider in this spot in 2011 how the copy is at once both creative and straight-speaking:

"Hey, here's a little good news. If you want decent mileage in a pick-up, you don't have to order your engine off the kiddie menu anymore. Say hello to variable-cam timing, direct injection and piston-cooling jets. Yeah. The engineers at Ford have been busy."

"Hey, here's a little good news. If you want decent mileage in a pick-up, you don't have to order your engine off the kiddie menu anymore. Say hello to variable cam timing, direct injection and piston cooling jets. Yeah. The engineers at Ford have been busy."

The result of telling the truth has been overwhelming. Sales in October 2010 were up 24 percent over the previous year, when the ads had just begun to seep into popular consciousness. Ford grew its share (already the largest) of the light- and heavy-duty truck market by 3.5 percentage points to 39 percent. Brand recognition for trucks averages 63 percent, yet Ford's F-150 rates at 72 percent. Not surprisingly, it committed to continuing the approach, and it's probably not complete coincidence that Chrysler's Ram truck division and GMC's Sierra developed their own campaigns based on service deals and other functional qualities of their offerings.

The result of telling the truth has been overwhelming. Sales in October 2010 were up 24 percent over the previous year, when the ads had just begun to seep into popular consciousness.

Ford's approach unified the normally divergent, if not overtly conflicted, aims of brand and sales-relevant marketing communications. Truth is what gave it that bridge. What is it about the particular challenge and opportunity for the F-150 that makes truth so effective? We see three broad qualities:

1. **Educated customers.** The criteria for truck purchases have always skewed to the functional, or rather, the emotional benefits of truck brands emerge from the various technical strengths of the products—big engines are better than smaller ones, and so forth. Because of this, Ford could assume that its audience was predisposed to such information, making telling them the truth less of a leap of faith than simply expanding on a prerequisite of communications. But it's not the same as throwing techno-jargon at an audience or playing to misconceptions. Facts that aren't understood aren't all that much better than pleasant lies, especially if they create the illusion of substance where no relevant substance exists. Neither holds up to the litmus tests of reality, especially over time.

2. **Likely repeat buyers.** It's a safe guess that the average truck owner has owned another truck sometime earlier up the road, so to speak. This prior experiential education means it's a lot harder to tell them things that aren't true, and a lot easier to presume they all know what they're looking for. A repeat buyer is also a textbook example of an advocate or a detractor (they'll either be repeat recommenders or critics), so an incentive for Ford (or for any truck manufacturer) is to keep things as declaratively simple and honest as possible. Too much creativity would detract from that positioning. Also, since truck owners are particularly vocal about their satisfaction or lack thereof, they're also a primary mechanism for referral and recommendation. The "rants" campaign talks to current owners as directly and honestly as it does to potential ones.

3. **Performance matters.** The ultimate test of a utility vehicle like a truck is how well it performs its duties—this is unlike vehicles in other categories that may or may not ever prove the relevance of engine size or suspension. As 24 Hour Fitness did in its truth campaign, Ford acknowledges this truth in its campaign by sticking to the functional benefits of its F-150 brand. Ram did the same when it promised in 2010 that "if it doesn't do everything you ask it to do, bring it back." Categories in which users have a closer relationship with the reality of their product performance are probably going to react better to functional marketing, irrespective of what you wish brands meant to them. Your marketing will be truthful only if it acknowledges reality, since that's what your customers will experience as owners.

Ford hit upon truth with its F-150 campaign and experienced success with it. This suggests to us that functional attributes could play a larger role in the content that other brands develop. Functional may not seem sexy on its face, but achieving results like Ford's sure seems pretty sexy in our book (pun intended).

Funny: Tire Tracks on His Shirt

Sometimes the truth of the matter can be stated in a way that brings laughter. Jokes and puns have a way of presenting the lighter side of reality. It's certainly no joke that Southwest Airlines has used the humorous side of truth to delight its patrons and reap the financial rewards of doing so.

The fates didn't seem inclined to give Southwest much of a break when it was a fledgling start-up in the early 1970s. Judges seemed intent on keeping the airline from ever taking off, and Herb Kelleher, its first general counsel and cofounder, spent much of his time fighting court battles. On June 17, 1971, he successfully got an injunction lifted that had literally grounded Southwest, and the company's president, Lamar Muse, asked him what the operations team should do if a sheriff showed up the next morning with another injunction. "Push the flight out over him, and leave tire tracks on his shirt," Kelleher replied. (Muse never had to try out the suggestion.)

Within the next few years, various parties would try to restrict Southwest from flying outside of Texas, through the courts and Congress, giving birth to the ten-minute turn; would try to force it to move from its close-to-downtown location at Dallas Love Field to the large DFW International Airport away from the city; repeatedly attempt to close the smaller airport entirely; and try to deny the no-frills carrier additional routes. Southwest overcame each and every setback.

Kelleher and the team had to laugh. Truly, it was the only way to survive. Also, this seemingly genetic need to be funny proved to be a way of delivering truth by helping its customers laugh, too. It has enabled Southwest to laugh all the way to the bank ever since.

The humorous approach started before the airline did. Rollin King, the other cofounder, studied the operations of Pacific Southwest Airlines (PSA), which presaged Southwest in a number of ways. A scrappy operation limited for most of its history to intrastate flights in California, PSA, "The World's Friendliest Airline," painted smiles on the noses of its planes and ran a TV spot in the early '70s with a "smile inspector" reviewing its in-flight crew (its advertising in the late '80s was called "Catch Our Smile"). It also dressed its stewardesses in miniskirts and ran many more commercials under the slogan, "PSA Gives You a Lift."

Southwest did much of the same thing early on. The airline's first recruitment ad for hostesses (not even stewardesses) read, "Attention, Raquel Welch: You can have a job if you measure up," and applicants were asked to wear hot pants to their interviews. Early classes of hostesses skewed heavily to former cheerleaders, and they were encouraged to display their special, er, personalities in the air. So many cases about Southwest's approach stop there, with the conscious playfulness, as if it were a conscious marketing strategy that delivered the brand. We think otherwise. The strategy, based in large part on PSA's pioneering work, was to generate awareness that far exceeded the attention an unknown start-up airline with limited routes and few marketing dollars could buy. And its branding also encouraged an esprit de corps that kept employees happy and motivated. The ads were funny, and they still are. (The 2010 television campaign ended with the line, "You are now free to move about the country.")

But there's truth underneath all of those uses.

Airline travel is such that if you don't laugh about it, you'll probably want to cry, especially if you're a regular or commuter traveler. You get up before the crack of dawn. You go through the insults of parking and airport security, then endure the waits and commensurate difficulties—and you haven't even set foot on an airplane yet! Seats are small and rows are tight, yet planes are packed. There's limited in-flight service, air turbulence, and crying babies. And after you land, you can look forward to more waiting and standing in line to get off the plane, and fighting traffic on the road before you eventually get to wherever it is you thought you wanted to go. The list and order of events change later in the day and also vary for leisure travelers, but the core indignities and unpleasantness are endemic to the experience.

Running funny ads and telling jokes just wouldn't cut it when compared to the reality of air travel (which is perhaps why so few of Southwest's competitors try it). Instead, Southwest's humor in the way it acknowledges reality and, in doing so, delivers truth in a way that no contrived comedy could do. When it laughs together with its passengers, it can't help but speak the truth, as if the brand is saying, "We know this is crazy but we can survive it together."

When it laughs together with its passengers, it can't help but speak the truth, as if the brand is saying, "We know this is crazy but we can survive it together."

The company doesn't tell its employees to be funny; they're simply told to be themselves. Be human beings. Don't shut off your empathy and awareness when you put on your Southwest uniform. "We never told them they can't be funny," a company spokesman explained. In this sense, its humor is far more genuine and truthful than any declaration of, "Your business is important to us" or, "We're sorry for the delay" exhortations that some other brand experience strategies specify. It's also important that the use of humor is not self-deprecating or snide. It's not used as a reference point about the brand experience or customer opinion; rather, it's a part of it. Southwest isn't laughing at itself or its customers, but it sure laughs with them about the reality of air travel.

It uses other tools to tell the truth, of course. It refused to follow the industry and charge for checked baggage and built a very effective marketing campaign based on this functional difference (it seemed more just and fair, which are qualities of truth). And its operational strategy of relying on point-to-point travel, which is mostly the result of being constrained by regulators early on, has continued to let it better manage its departures and arrivals schedule—and its operating margins.

Southwest has delivered thirty-eight consecutive years of profitability and has consistently outperformed its rivals. Those truly stellar results are no laughing matter.

Here are a few ways to think about humor as the content for truth:

- **Don't be too smart.** You can have a smart, consciously funny commercial and yet still miss the boat. This is because a lot of the humor in ads and viral videos doesn't rise to the level of truth. It's just entertainment. What Southwest does is allow its staff, from in-flight personnel to its marketers, to share their human reaction to their work, which often comes in the form of humor. Don't overthink it.

- **Don't be crude.** Speaking of viral videos, isn't it odd that the humor in so many of them seems to be blunt or just plain gross, as if consumers will pay attention only if something surprises or offends? There's no way your brand can own a fart joke or the latest in an endless iteration of sexist pranks, so there's nothing truthful about it (other than that most of it is truly awful).

- **Do be involving.** For humor to be the content of truth, the "joke" has to be shared with brand and consumer; it needs to be a laugh that they have together over some aspect of their communal experience or circumstance.

Fair: You Know You Have Something to Say

Most people don't want to have to think about both sides of an argument. It's an evolutionary imperative: when faced with a saber-toothed tiger in the wilderness, it does you absolutely no good to be thinking about how hungry the beast must be. You don't think about the two sides to the story. You simply run and you run fast. Accuracy, fairness, and even truth don't factor into many such instances. It's like that old joke about the bear and the sports shoes. Two men are walking in the woods and see a bear rampaging toward them. One of them stops to put on his athletic shoes and the second man says to him, "Why are you bothering to do that? You can't outrun a bear." The first one replies, "I don't need to outrun the bear. I only need to be faster than you."

The point in most arguments isn't to grow or learn the subtle nuances of others' opinions—it's to win. We pick the side we want to go for and look for more reasons to stick to it and, when that fails, we opt for attacking our opponents personally. This is how politics usually works and why outspoken radio talk show hosts gain audiences. It is not easy to change people's opinions, so few actually try (which is why many so-called "conversations" are more like linear "versations" of one opinion following the last).

However, there is also another human instinct, which is appreciation of *congruity*. We like things to make sense and if we're presented convincingly enough with two sides of a story, we will listen and try to unify or coordinate them with one another. Think less overt advocacy, which often falls on deaf ears, and more collaborative, or additive (as we discuss elsewhere in this chapter). It's easy to tell people what you think they *should* know; it's quite another thing to actually involve them in a conversation about what they *want* to talk about, and which has any hope of presenting truths and changing their opinions of them. So when energy company E.ON really needed to change opinions in the United Kingdom, it took the unexpected step of creating truly real conversations with its target market.

E.ON is one of the United Kingdom's leading energy suppliers and in 2009 was facing a number of challenges. None of them were unique to E.ON. How green is it? Are the prices it charges fair? How can it improve reliability, which, in E.ON's case, meant decreasing the likelihood of power brownouts or blackouts? It did have a few unique challenges, too, mostly that electricity is an "invisible" product provided by a utility-like service that is only interesting when it breaks down or violates the rules. The challenge was how to overcome these many obstacles and gain the edge over its rivals as truly customer focused.

Catherine Woolfe had joined E.ON as head of advertising and brand strategy from Volkswagen. In her previous job, she had the benefit of a product that most consumers desire and of an advertising heritage to which many marketers aspire. VW's UK advertising has won award after award over the last decade. Woolfe's raw materials at E.ON were quite different: smaller budgets, invisible product, no advertising heritage, and a controversial sector.

She immediately created a new team around her, calling first a media pitch and then a creative agency pitch. The new integrated team needed to drive E.ON's communications to start to make inroads into an intractable problem—to make E.ON stand out from the crowd by creating a distinct and attractive brand to an indifferent audience. The opportunity was no less than to "give E.ON a new face," with the overall objective of persuading people to choose an energy company for reasons that were not just commodity price-based decisions.

Woolfe started from a basic personal truth, which she described as, "If my energy company treats me like a commodity, I will treat it like one back." This came directly out of the mouth of a lady in a research focus group and had stuck with Woolfe ever since. The team was briefed to treat the target market like well-informed adults. The idea, originating from the creative agency DLKW's pitch, was to have a real-life conversation with the British public about the issues involved in energy consumption—not to pat them on the head and not to patronize them but to be intelligent and accessible. Sounds like arguing for motherhood and apple pie, right? Well, it was what many brands tried to do, or told themselves they were trying to do. Making it happen was an entirely other matter.

Woolfe had a secret weapon at the ready. She'd been inspired by an account of a public relations lunch told to her by Guy Esnouf, E.ON's head of PR and public affairs. For once, E.ON had broken with the normal way of doing stakeholder engagement, which was to invite one interest group at a time in for a conversation. This time, however, the green, business, and poverty lobbies were invited together. Instead of E.ON hosting an audience that would attend just to attack it and require the company to offer defenses in a two-way debate, it enabled a real conversation among various interests in which it was a participant or even a mediator. This elevated the discussion of truths beyond the typical "you said/I said" bickering and allowed for real engagement.

This was especially useful because energy production and consumption are more complicated than we would like them to be. You can have cheap electricity, but it is unlikely to be perfectly carbon-neutral. You can go all out and deliver green electricity, but it may well be unreliable or expensive (and vulnerable consumers need their electricity to be cheap and reliable). These three basic challenges formed the "Trilemma" that E.ON's campaign sought to address, by involving consumers in debate and getting them to start formulating the answers for themselves.

Nick Jefferies, the account director at the newly appointed media agency, was very up for encouraging debate. The whole direction of his team's work had been driven by thinking about communications planning in the twenty-first century as a way to encourage positive conversations among consumers instead of simply sticking advertisements in front of them. Their thinking on the brief was to create a hub for a debate by creating content, putting it in a public space, and allowing the conversations among different opinion formers to drive a wide-reaching argument involving thousands of people. With agencies DLKW and Grand Union, the campaign that was developed went far further than any "tell" advertising campaign could, into a campaign that would push the consumer to think about the issues involved.

In other words, they decided to form an agnostic, open community, and the E.ON Trilemma campaign was born.

The team, again working with the E.ON press office, created

a channel on YouTube fueled by three initial videos that put forward the arguments separately for low-carbon, low-cost, and reliable electricity. With media partner *The Telegraph* (the biggest broadsheet daily newspaper in the United Kingdom) and long radio commercials, a campaign to promote the debate drove hundreds of thousands of viewings. Positive attitudes toward the company doubled without it ever propagandizing its own points of view. Woolfe says that the truth was one of the only things that could have made this change in attitude happen. Never mind that this truth wasn't simple, one-dimensional, or even conclusive. The energy problem remains unresolved and will so for the foreseeable future. All that we can hope is that well-intentioned people will work on finding the answers, and it's on this truth—complicated and messy as it is in this case—that E.ON gave its brand a voice that would not be ignored.

Forecasted: Credit for Making the Effort

The possibility of moving one of England's bank holidays to October because there are just too many clustered in spring comes up every few years or so. However, the discussion never goes anywhere because the weather in October, while reasonably mild, is never predictable. So plans for a new holiday—such as Battle of Trafalgar Day (a tribute to the impressive win by the British Royal Navy against Napoleon in 1805) or something equally memorable—stay on the drawing board, never implemented. People direct their hopes and fears to spring holidays that in actuality offer no better guarantee of nice weather.

Talking about the weather was the top British trait in a survey of five thousand adults published in *The Telegraph* newspaper in 2008 (being good at queuing and a love of sarcasm came in, somewhat intriguingly, second and third, respectively). Clearly, the lack of properly defined seasons is partly at fault, as the idea of a regular rainy season would strike most British people as laughable (it would essentially extend all year). The one thing they know for certain is that the weather will let them down. They plan for the best and expect the worst, which can often mean making indoor plans.

Their suspicions are borne out by the science of meteorology. One website researched forecasting accuracy in late 2010 by correlating two weeks' worth of predictions and actual local weather conditions. Their most positive finding was that the BBC, Met Office (the UK National Weather Service), and The Weather Channel performed much better than taking random guesses. The best of the three delivered 57 percent accuracy, which is a hit rate that we think would stun most people. And the funny thing about probability and human perception is that 50 percent gets interpreted as no different from making no prediction whatsoever. A fifty-fifty chance of good or bad weather is not an insight upon which you can plan an outdoor wedding, boating trip, or enhancement to your tan.

The weather in England is notoriously unpredictable, yet we still check the weather forecasts, even in light of some stunning examples of forecasters getting it wrong—such as Michael Fish and the hurricane prediction of 1987. The day of one of the worst storms in living memory, when trees were uprooted and homes extensively damaged, Fish had read the weather forecast on BBC TV and said reassuringly, "Earlier on today, apparently, a woman rang the BBC and said she heard there was a hurricane on the way; well, if you're watching, don't worry, there isn't. . . ." Unfortunately for Fish, what followed was the worst storm in more than two hundred years.

More recently, in spring of 2009, there was a very confident report of a "Barbeque Summer," but by July one man was being blamed for "stealing our summer." The culprit was Met Office's Chief Meteorologist Ewen McCallum, who'd made comments to tabloid newspapers that April ". . . should be seeing some good hot spells and perhaps get the old barbeque out."

What we find interesting is that McCallum batted away at criticisms for being proven wrong. Speaking to James Orr at the *Mirror* at the end of July 2009, he reminded everyone by saying: "Clearly not every forecast will be right otherwise we'd be God. This is an advice service. People have got to understand we're only giving advice. It's not like we've built a car and the wheels have fallen off. . . ." Orr concludes, "Despite the data gathering and all the computing power money can buy, the Met Office's forecasts are only forecasts and no more, not promises." Truer words were never spoken, and they speak to the centrality of truth even in the face of being imperfect. What is true can be wrong as well as right and, in the case of weather forecasting, the content can be wrong without being misleading or false. Truth transcends those qualities.

British consumers know this when it comes to the weather (as do residents in other countries, of course). No matter how wrong the forecast is on any particular occasion, people return to it time and again for two reasons. First, it's better than nothing. They, like the forecasters, need to collect as much information as they can in order to make the best decisions possible. Forecasts are inputs to this process, and because they make no pretense of replacing other inputs, including consumers' own cynicism, they are accepted at face value. We think this quality also makes them true.

The second reason, which has major implications for any brand's communications with the public, is that people understand, perhaps intuitively, the basis on which the predictions are made. They know that there are no guarantees, so they cannot bank on their accuracy. But they know too that the people working up the forecasts are trying their best to be accurate and that they are trying their best to be helpful.

At no point does the Met Office or any other forecast

provider make a promise it cannot keep. This unspoken contract with the public hoping for sunshine is that, together, they know they may well be doomed. They'll share the best possible advice and expect the worst. Most people's expectation of a forecast in the United Kingdom is for "sunny spells with the possibility of showers" alternating with "showers with sunny intervals." Either forecast will likely be wrong, but the effort of forecasting speaks with the inalterable voice of truth.

LESS TIME

The first TV commercial debuted in the United States early in the afternoon on July 1, 1941. The Brooklyn Dodgers and Philadelphia Phillies were about to play a game that would be broadcast on WNBT in New York, which had signed on air that day as the first commercially licensed TV station in America. The commercial showed a map of the United States, over which an image of a clock appeared and a voice intoned, "America runs on Bulova time." The spot lasted twenty seconds. It cost Bulova nine dollars. The game would last about three hours.

Talk about a momentary absence from, or of, reality.

Whether entertainment or commercial content, the history of media experiences is that they were often detached from viewers' circumstances. That Bulova message had three hours to sink in! Granted, it wasn't necessarily memorable, but what's important is to understand how easily and frequently marketers had the latitude to avoid acknowledging reality (and how much time was available for it). Just contrast that experience with

(continued on next page)

(continued from previous page)

how quickly a brand truth today is put to the test. Not hours. Not even minutes, necessarily. Often it's almost immediately. Technology and culture have conspired to make acknowledging reality almost a requirement if you aspire to communicate truth, as the lack thereof will be instantly obvious to your consumer. And lack of truth is indeed a lie, in one way or another.

Conclusion

Acknowledging reality seems like such a "duh" quality of communicating truth, but we all know that so much of brand marketing is intended to take consumers away from reality. As marketers, the truths we convey are somehow above and separate from the messy circumstances in which people experience, absorb, share, and ultimately act upon the information we share with them; our challenge is to insert into this chaos our brand positions that will withstand and survive the onslaught of reality.

Our thesis is that brands should do the exact opposite. They should acknowledge reality in their content *before* consumers do it for them. Because—trust us—they will.

This quality of truth applies to the biggest strategy as much as it merits attention in the smallest tactical element. However, there are at least three operational pitfalls you will want to consider when you try to apply this thinking to your next meeting:

1. **Lies by omission.** We've all seen the beautiful vacation-destination marketing: images of pristine beaches and hotel pools empty of people in which a couple frolics

and is demographically similar to us (only lots thinner and prettier). There's a defensible reason why this branding still dominates a lot of travel marketing, but we think it risks not just coming across as irrelevantly idealized but simply false. If your creative idea requires that you conceptually white out core components of reality, you should perhaps rethink the strategy. Aspirations can quickly become empty (untruthful) when consumers correlate your promise with their past experiences (or experiences that are shared within their social networks).

2. **Be present.** Like the Bulova commercial in the 1940s, most marketing used to exist in a comfortable vacuum, a momentary suspension of disbelief or requirements of veracity that you could call a "brand pause." There was time for promises of better, happier, easier, and more economical lives to be absorbed, most times without immediate challenge. Brand marketing could afford to talk about reality as if it were somewhere or sometime else. Something to be laughed at or mocked. Oftentimes it didn't reference reality at all (much of entertainment marketing is purposefully so). The nature of truth in today's marketplace is that your brand has no such latitude; worse, if you practice the old habits of entertainment and spin, you risk seeming disconnected or disjointed from real experience. Such disconnects also suggest falsehood.

3. **Answer the questions.** Another quality of the immediacy of consumer experience is that you can be sure that some element of the past will be included in the present. No moment today can be completely separate from other moments, whether historical or concurrent. Our technology and, as a result, our expectations are such that every *now* is connected to a *when* and many times also to a *then*. For your communications to be truthful,

you need to anticipate this context and preemptively address it. You can also choose to avoid it altogether, but be sensitive to point number one above. If it's an obvious question you're avoiding, you won't escape it and your content will be deemed false. There's more on the importance of context in Chapter Seven.

Acknowledging reality is a huge creative challenge, perhaps more so than coming up with ideas without such constraints. But we believe we've shared some cases with you that make the argument for stepping up just this sort of challenge. Can you apply one or more of the tools to your next strategy? We think so, especially if you remind yourself and your team that the starting point for successful brands and marketing communication isn't a fantasy, image, or belief. It's truth. If your content acknowledges truth, it'll be more believable, which, in turn, could make it more effective. Do it better than your competition and you'll have a presence in your marketplace that works to your advantage.

ACKNOWLEDGE REALITY CHECKLIST

Each chapter has a set of checklists that will enable you to judge how you're doing against each of the ways of delivering brand truth. Work through them as honestly as you can and you will find ways to gain a competitive advantage. Here's the Acknowledge Reality Checklist to start the ball rolling.

1. Which is the most straight-talking brand in your category? If it isn't yours, then what can you do to change that?

2. Is there a truth about the category that no brand owns? If so, can you find a way to own it first (like Southwest has on low prices and no-hassle pricing)?

3. Is there a truth that you know but traditionally work to avoid? If so, could you turn it into an opportunity for your brand by addressing it?

4. Can you own up to something—a lack of omniscience, for example—that will give you more credibility in the future?

5. How much of your past year's worth of business operations and marketing communications is reflected in your plans for next year? How consistent are you? Can you improve that number?

6. Is there something that most customers hate about the category? What can you do to mitigate it?

7. How can you show your customers that you regard them as intelligent equals in your marketing?

8. How much of your brand communication reflects what your competitors communicate versus what your business delivers? Can you shift the content onto the latter?

9. If you had to step back from the brand promises you make, let's say by a third, in terms of absolute numbers and conviction of your presentation, what would those changes be? Could you deliver better understanding by claiming fewer benefits but making their delivery more likely and sustainable?

10. Who is the "reality check" person in your department? Is there someone who possesses the authority and review processes to serve as your arbiter of what's truthful or not? You might want to consider giving someone the duties.

2

Deliver Real Change to Services and Company Structure

What you do is as important as what you say. While this might seem like an obvious truth, the advent of social media has made this an urgent consideration in an unprecedented way.

Much has been written and said about the emergence of social media technologies and their role in marketing. The two of us blog and tweet, and we used the Internet to collaborate on this book, so we're users as well as fans. Not only did social media help us create this work but the findings of our book—the centrality of truth—certainly also apply to social tools, just as they do to an entire range of brand and marketing functions. We don't mean to give social media short shrift, however. The real relevance and import of social media technology (the advent of the Internet and its related sites, programs, and apps) is not that it is controversial, in and of itself, but that it allows us to see that *every* media channel and platform is conversational. This is a huge realization, in part because it challenges us to see every marketing function and activity as components of customer service. They always were, really, it's just that we didn't always look at them that way. We think that fully embracing this point of view is an important tool for defining your content. We want to spend some time looking at how conversation and customer service are related, and how this can make telling the truth a service, too.

Consumers have always talked about brands. Conversation was a behavior long before there were technology tools to enable and support it, and it's not just the way by which people share, vet, recommend, and affirm their choices, but the way that societies are run. These dialogues are two-way (or multi-way, more accurately) and they've occurred ever since people wore togas or knickers with knee-high socks. The primary way businesses contributed to these conversations was through performance (the experiences that products and services provided), if not through the simple availability of their wares in communities in which there were few to no choices. This changed in the twentieth century, when communities developed greater economic well-being (which created demand for more choices and more things), and media technologies allowed businesses to remotely contribute to consumer conversations with branding (the artifacts of marketing communications). The output of branding—"content," though it wasn't classified as such until much more recently—was generally assumed to be either true, because there were limited ways to prove or share findings of inaccuracy, or presumed to be irrelevantly funny and entertaining, so affirmation or denial of truthfulness wasn't even an issue. Brands were stand-ins for experience, only distantly created and shared.

Not so much anymore. The advent of social media technologies has brought with it consumer conversations that are more frequent, often more substantive, usually occur in real time, and have a very immediate here-and-now quality. It's no surprise that consumers' trust in corporate statements has declined as their use of social tools has increased; engagement makes them more aware and potentially more critical of the content that brands have traditionally provided. While it has gotten easier for brands to share content directly with consumers (to act as direct participants in conversations), it has gotten harder for those efforts to be accepted as authentic or true. What were once authoritative declarations are now "branded content" that is added to their ongoing conversations with consumers as another data point or opinion. Many brand campaigns avoid having their truths judged in these conversations by creating entertainment, just like brands did a half-century ago, or outsourcing their creations entirely to "the crowd." Conversation, and not truth, has been dubbed an "absolute good."

As you'll see throughout the first half of this book, we believe that the path to achieving truth isn't to declare it, no matter how creatively it might be digitally delivered to your consumers' consciousness. Instead, today the mandate for brands is to submit, suggest, enable, clarify, forward, support, and otherwise encourage conversation, less *with* itself and more *about* it. Consumers today are more likely (and better empowered) to determine the truth for themselves than at any time in history. This has made everything a business does a contribution to the ongoing dialogue, and it renders measures of engagement or frequency less important than the subsequent uses and sustainability of it. All of your marketing activities add to this dialogue. Your Facebook page is a part of it. So are your instructional or entertaining videos, as are your billboards and press releases. How you treat your employees and vendors contributes to the conversation. You get the idea. The truth that emerges from this dialogue is less a reaction to your brand communications than it is an outcome of the conversations your customers have *about* it.

Today, the mandate for brands is to submit, suggest, enable, clarify, forward, support, and otherwise encourage conversation, less with itself and more about it. Consumers today are more likely (and better empowered) to determine the truth for themselves than at any time in history.

This changed quality of how truth is defined requires a change in how you approach its development. We think a useful model for understanding this is to consider a "process of truth"—the enablement of truth versus the declaration of it—that is somewhat similar to what customer service used to be. Consider it the first *post-Twitter service strategy.*

You've seen this reality emerge as a driver of the success of online media aggregators like *The Huffington Post* and *The Daily Beast,* which have been extensively dissected to understand how they applied processes of truth-telling to their business models, and thereby replaced the declarations that traditional journalism once made. It's been apparent not only in technology tools like Twitter but also in the customer service forums (both public and private) that many technology brands have created.

We want to dive deeper and look at different examples to understand what's really going on.

First, please indulge us with a little history. Before social tools like blogs came along, there were few avenues available for disappointed consumers to express their dismay or other feelings about a product or experience. Letters could be written, sent, and then mostly ignored or forgotten, and few businesses kept track of anyone who wasn't a chronic complainer. People could tell family and friends of their experiences, who could then pass that information to their own contacts, but the resulting ripple effect was somewhat limited and short-lived. Conversely, it wasn't uncommon for businesses to ignore complaints, or sometimes prove unable to fix whatever had caused consumers to be unsatisfied. The primary mechanism dissatisfied customers used for expressing their feelings was to literally "vote with their pocketbooks" and stop buying whatever product or service had let them down. It was an imperfect system, but it worked. It was also an ongoing conversation, albeit one that was slow and imprecise by our standards.

The only real and meaningful tool that businesses had at their disposal was customer service, which encompassed not just the back end of broken user experiences but included every aspect of the brand-consumer conversation leading up to it. Department stores and airlines had "complaint departments," but customer service was a broad function that incorporated much of what the business made and sold. Again, it certainly wasn't perfect or complete, but brands had to be prepared for their customers to contact them since they didn't have the proactive capacity to reach out and touch them often. Customer service wasn't "problem fixing" as much as it was "problem avoiding." Perhaps consumers were less dissatisfied with brands in the past not because they didn't have the capacity to complain but because brands did a better job of providing customer service that prevented problems in the first place and therefore avoided any gulf between brand image and service delivery? Perhaps expectations were better matched to outcomes because the ongoing communications were simply more *true?*

In this sense, the truth of those earlier brands was declared by their gloriously one-way marketing efforts, but then it was substantiated by the ongoing behaviors of the business. There was an inherent integrity to these dialogues because they were based on a shared understanding of what was possible and what was likely. Again, do not mistake this as a value judgment about whether the conversation was fair or appropriate or not, though to the vast majority of participants it was both. It was as much limited by the ability or willingness to make wild promises as it was by the shortcomings of the technologies through which the dialogues occurred. But however imperfectly, truth happened at the meeting of brand delivery and customer receipt. It came from the ongoing nature of the conversation, not just its conclusion or from something that brands declared.

Now fast-forward again to our present. Every brand publishes content and maintains various conversations with its consumers. These behaviors are not necessarily synonymous with communicating truth. We've found that the brands accomplishing the most when it comes to being truthful often do so by embracing these somewhat more traditional perspectives on conversation and customer communication. So it's not "new rules" of behavior that yield better relationships but rather new ways of applying the "old rules."

Successful brands configure their internal operations (primarily marketing departments) to approach the totality of service as a function of their brands, not a component of them, and they engage their consumers in ongoing conversations that are not exclusively about the brands themselves but about the consumers' experience of them. This yields sustainable and effective relationships based on truth—a true understanding of what the brand is doing, how it does it, and why it matters. Again, we see two broad ways brands deliver on this idea of "truth as a service":

> *Successful brands configure their internal operations (primarily marketing departments) to approach the totality of service as a function of their brands, not a component of them, and they engage their consumers in ongoing conversations that are not exclusively about the brands themselves but about the consumers' experience of them.*

- **The processes in which your brand engages *internally*.** How are your internal participants—your employees—tasked and focused? These are the ways you set up every service to be a way of telling the truth instead of all the imaginative, declarative platforms that normally define brand strategies.

- **The processes in which your brand engages *externally*.** How do you outsource and collaborate on facts with your consumers? Why should consumers have any involvement with your content beyond entertainment or passing curiosity? How can you manage your interaction with the consumer to yield truth? This will be the most important strategic idea behind any conversation you might prompt or in which your brand participates.

We will spend this chapter exploring in great detail some examples that you've not heard all that much about, so as to reveal the qualities of these "internal" and "external" processes of delivering truth as a service.

Internal: Call Centers *Are* the Brand

When did call centers first come into our lives? There was a time when customer calls with complaints or issues into a business were considered one of the many activities that constituted overall service. Like the "voice of the customer" in the statistical controls of business operators, it was a source of insight as well as an opportunity to strengthen brand relationships.

Things began to change in America in the 1950s, with the idea that this component of service was a cost center ripe for better management; the truth of listening to the customer's voice was that doing so was an expense, and the creation of call centers was intended to drive efficiency in minimizing it. In the United Kingdom, they really took off in the 1970s and became an omnipresent function a decade later. Today, they are the bedrock of some businesses and the origin of two of the United Kingdom's best-known brands.

Yet the story is still being written. This case is about two brands, both of which were born from the idea of call centers, that have evolved to be web- and telephone-based, and which are now looking to reaffirm the truth of service as a builder of brand relationships and value by making real changes to how their crucial call centers operate. These brands are considering throwing away efficiencies in the shape of call center scripts and precise time targets in order to improve the value of the brands to the customer and to the shareholder.

In 1985, Peter Wood launched Direct Line, the first United Kingdom company to exclusively sell insurance over the telephone. By 1990, TV ads featuring a cheerful animated red telephone with wheels (because the core product at launch was car insurance) sold the idea of cutting out the middleman (the broker) for cost savings on what essentially remains a low-interest yet compulsory purchase. Direct Line started out with just sixty-three employees, and for years its main driver of growth was the switch from brokers to direct buys of insurance over the phone. Its call centers have remained UK-based. It is one of the leading United Kingdom brands and, for a while, it had the UK direct insurance market to itself.

But success breeds competitors, and today most British car drivers wouldn't know how to buy insurance other than direct by phone or on the Internet. All of the big UK insurance businesses created brands for the direct marketplace.

One brand in particular was launched specifically to compete with Direct Line—Churchill Insurance. It was created in 1989 by Martin Long, who had been involved in the launch of Direct Line four years earlier. Where Direct Line had a red phone as its advertising and brand logo—one that brilliantly helped to explain how to buy the product in those early days when people had to be persuaded out of high street insurance broker shops—Churchill adopted its iconic bulldog as the result of a staff competition in 1994. The nodding dog and his catchphrase, "Oh, Yes," when asked if he can save the consumer money, is a key feature of the TV advertising and is greatly loved in the United Kingdom. In the last couple of years the dog has even appeared in pantomime at Christmas throughout the land.

Now, the brands are no longer run by rival companies but are both owned by RBSi, the largest home and motor insurance company in the United Kingdom. The marketing operations are now linked, and because the companies are run on a direct-to-consumer basis via the phone and web, there is a huge amount of analysis, understanding, and accountability for marketing that is second to none.

But the brand's marketing isn't just the advertising with phones on red wheels or animated dogs, as Crawford

Davidson, the UK marketing chief, knows only too well. He's prepared to spend significant sums of money—millions of pounds—to change the service delivery of the brands he runs for the better, and to better differentiate between them.

Despite the pulling together of much of the backroom delivery of the two brands over the last five years, the differences in customer perception have remained strong. This is, of course, renewed constantly by the different advertising approach of the two brands. But Davidson dates the different brand perceptions back to the early days of Churchill and first noticed them when he was running a different brand altogether at Tesco Personal Finance:

> I was at TPF between '03 and '06. Direct Line was a big competitor, but Churchill was outperforming in terms of customer satisfaction scores. It's obvious now that the founder had created something very valuable in terms of culture at Churchill that was focused on the customer . . . the service ethos meant that staff would go to great lengths to get things right for customers . . . they would send a bunch of flowers if a customer had had a really rotten day and if deserved apologies would be not just rational but emotional too.

Now, this can be difficult in an insurance company. They need to be good at paying out the right claims to the customer—not more or less—because if you pay less, you'll eventually lose the customer, but if you pay more, then it will end up driving up overall pricing to everyone.

But there is something about the differences still between Direct Line and Churchill customers that definitely warrants a different approach to all forms of customer contact. Unlike Churchill customers, Direct Line customers don't want an emotional or overpersonalized service. They tend to be very self-sufficient and mostly prefer to deal with the company via the Internet for nearly everything. They want the technology to work and to work well.

Churchill customers, however, want people to talk to. The differences are not just about demographics, although they tend to be older and wealthier. The typical Churchill customer likes to have everything explained to them and not to be hurried. It is a truth that the entire marketing team constantly strives to keep in mind.

This reality is obviously at odds with a system that seeks to drive efficiencies and to standardize procedures. But it is absolutely crucial to the team's ethos of delivering the best for shareholders as well as colleagues and customers. Davidson himself regularly experiences what it is like in the thick of things in the call centers because, together with the rest of the executive team, he does several days a year in a center himself and always asks to be given the difficult customer calls to answer personally. Along with dealing with the calls, he talks to the other employees who are manning the phones. They've told him directly that they are ambivalent about moving immediately from representing the Churchill brand in one call to representing the Direct Line brand in the next.

"The call center staff themselves say that they feel a bit disingenuous having a Churchill conversation one minute and then a Direct Line one," Davidson said.

Given that his two brands are the top two in the sector for consumers, Davidson sees it as the marketing team's responsibility to ensure that the brands live up to customer expectations. There is profit in doing so in his view, too. A recent research meeting uncovered very clearly that although Churchill customers will say that they buy on price, more probing indicates that they mean they buy the best-priced "good" insurance brand that they can. So they will actually pay more for the Churchill brand delivery.

When the car needs a repair, Churchill customers aren't necessarily in a hurry to get the car back.

Said Davidson:

> When the call centers talk to customers about how quickly we can get their repaired car back to them, a Direct Line customer will assume a quality-assured service and is interested in speed of delivery. With a Churchill customer, if you stress speed then they start to worry about the quality of the repair. Speed actually gives the customer a problem—they question whether it will be done properly.

Research also shows that a different length of conversation is required—Direct Line customers like quick and efficient conversations. Churchill customers want to talk more and want assistance and advice.

Out of all of this came the current pilot—one that it is hoped will deliver not only improvements in the brand's image but also in profitability.

Instead of closely controlling the call center with one standardized script and budgeted time spent on the phone, the company decided to explain the outcomes that it wants to call handlers, leaving the time spent and what they say (outside of the statutory legal requirements) mostly up to them. It was a revolution for the image of call centers, which doesn't usually conjure up the idea of empowered employees.

Instead of closely monitoring the call times, the business moved to measuring the outcomes. The initial results were overwhelmingly positive: overall call lengths went down and not up, yet the teams sold more services, answered more calls, and converted better. In addition, call center colleagues reported that they felt more positive and happier. For the long-termers (25 percent of the workforce have been there ten years or more), this is a joyous return to the days when they simply represented one brand or the other.

The business is convinced that the way forward is to make sure that the service the customer receives in every respect better matches the brand promise. As Davidson put it, the company is "allowing the staff to be true to themselves. When you talk to the call center people, they will talk about being Direct Line or Churchill with incredible pride. And personally they are different. Direct Line [workers] have more assertion. Churchill people are more empathetic. It's genuinely there."

These changes are not slight. The call centers employ more than ten thousand people in the United Kingdom. Treating them as adults rather than as instruments so they can define the truth of the brands' relationship with policyholders by their sanctioned actions, not just the happy words of marketing, is a revolutionary move in our view, and the initial quantitative results support our premise that it makes for better, stronger, and more profitable business operations.

Collaborating, Not Just Commenting

The Guardian is one of the most visible and engaged media properties online, and it's not a coincidence. Alan Rusbridger has been the newspaper's editor since 1995 and has dedicated years to developing its digital credentials, transforming it from a solid printed newspaper product mainly sold and read in the United Kingdom to one of the world's leading liberal voices online. In the process, Rusbridger (who came of age in the world of traditional print) became one of the leading proponents and practitioners of "citizen journalism," making *The Guardian* a leader in the way it uses the open source contributions of ordinary people to drive its investigative journalism.

Like police officers, journalists have always sought to

uncover sources of information by interrogating bystanders of incidents. America's Watergate story wouldn't have been told had Deep Throat not been interviewed by Woodward and Bernstein. There is a long tradition of detectives, both fictional and real, soliciting information from informants through a variety of creative means. But *The Guardian* has institutionalized a new tradition of recruiting ordinary citizens as journalists to contribute evidence to stories, and to vet the truth from fiction.

Not all of this truth is palatable or unique. *The Guardian's* "Comment Is Free" sections allow unlimited anonymous online comments about selected features. Although the contributors are, to a certain extent, self-selecting by personality and political persuasion, the substance and flow of the comments do not always suit the journalist authors of the original pieces. Rusbridger acknowledged this in his speech at the 2010 Cudlipp Lecture, saying, "There are lots of concerns … not least the ignorant, relentlessly negative, sometimes hate-filled tone of some of what you get back when you open the doors." In other words, *The Guardian's* experience with open comments isn't unlike that of most media outlets; unmoderated "conversation" often defaults to "versation" of one angry comment after another, usually referencing comments prior and not necessarily the prompting story. Just as this isn't unique, it's not indicative of any truth (or a truth that falls within the purview of this book, although students of human behavior should have a field day with it).

There has been significant disagreement among the professional journalists within *The Guardian* about how far the product should be opened up to its readers. In the spring of 2010, a series of breakfast meetings was held at the newspaper's headquarters to debate the extent to which each part of the newspaper could be opened up to involve readers. One insider explained that, for example, sports journalists, especially soccer writers, were very open to including debate from their readers, arguing that a lifelong soccer fan will have a level of devoted expertise (as well as passion) about his own team with which a general sports journalist could not hope to compete. The business journalists felt very differently, seeing their jobs as being the experts and not the moderators of ranting opinions from impassioned fans of one stock or another. Comments sections are "external space" in which spectators can be heard, even if mostly by themselves. They're a work in progress, to be sure.

> *Sports journalists, especially soccer writers, were very open to including debate from their readers, arguing that a lifelong soccer fan will have a level of devoted expertise (as well as passion) about his own team with which a general sports journalist could not hope to compete.*

It is in the area of investigative journalism more than anywhere else that *The Guardian* is justly proud of its record in uncovering story after story by encouraging public contributions, and thereby inventing a new process of truth-telling that it has embraced internally. In 2009, reporter Paul Lewis wrote a story entitled, "Citizen Journalism Counters Police Propaganda" that encapsulated this process.

Ian Tomlinson was a London newspaper vendor who died of a heart attack on his way home from work. The initial explanation of his death was made tragic because it appeared that he'd been unintentionally caught up in a fracas prompted when anarchist rioters attacked police during the G20 protests. In New York a few days later, a hedge fund manager who had attended the demonstrations out of curiosity while on a business trip read the account of Tomlinson's death, and the story did not match his own memory of events. He'd seen Tomlinson hit and had footage taken with a small digital camera to prove it. Within twenty-four hours, *The Guardian* had broadcast on its website the man's video taken of the incident showing that Tomlinson had been assaulted by a man in uniform. Eventually his assailant came forward and a criminal inquiry was launched.

In early 2011, British members of Parliament called for an inquiry into the death of a prisoner who had collapsed while being deported from the United Kingdom by a private security firm. Witnesses on the plane contacted *The Guardian* and their testimony contesting the official reports led to an investigation by Scotland Yard and a review of the whole system of deportation from the United Kingdom. Rusbridger sees such processes for finding truth as an extension of what newspapers have always been about, saying, in the Cudlipp Lecture:

> There is an irreversible trend in society today, about how people are expressing themselves, about how societies will choose to organize themselves, about a new democracy of ideas and information, about changing notions of authority, about the releasing of individual creativity, about an ability to hear previously unheard voices, about respecting, including, and harnessing the views of others. About resisting the people who want to close down free speech.

Here's how we see Rusbridger's philosophy put into a process of defining truth:

- **Engagement with purpose.** *The Guardian* defines its engagement as something more than reader reaction and aspires to citizen participation. Most local television stations and newspapers solicit tips and snippets of video (it's why we see footage of storm damage almost nightly), but *The Guardian* goes beyond such offers to incorporate citizens into codevelopment of the truths it presents. Less reaction and more collaborative action.

- **Vetting of facts.** In a world in which everyone's opinion is newsworthy, it's hard for one media property to differentiate itself from any other by simply repurposing this content. Asking for opinions isn't enough, especially if the brand is hoping to achieve an understanding of the truth. *The Guardian* goes further and defines what and how it wants to engage with its readers. What it risks losing in nuance or emotion it gains in giving readers specific tasks to accomplish, thereby keeping its experience "open" by limiting the participation that tends to "close down" conversation and engagement.

- **Qualified participation.** Asking an anonymous reader how the government should structure its economic policy might generate a colorful response, but will likely move the conversation closer to a collection of opinions and not to a shared truth (unless the question chanced upon an economics professor overqualified to give an answer). *The Guardian* instead defines its engagement with a purpose and then empowers it to achieve greater clarity and truth. You can't open source truth, but you can use open source tools to get closer to it.

We would say that this makes *The Guardian* a product that is full of truth.

External: In Open Communities, Truth Is an Orphan

It seemed reasonable enough. It was March 2010, and a huge tsunami had caused major damage at Japan's Fukushima

Daiichi nuclear power plant and devastated the northern part of the country. News reports of radiation leaks and the possibility of core meltdowns concerned people around the world; it was hard to find someone who didn't have an opinion about it. The blogosphere was buzzing with posts and conversations.

News reports of radiation leaks and the possibility of core meltdowns concerned people around the world; it was hard to find someone who didn't have an opinion about it. The blogosphere was buzzing with posts and conversations.

One post argued that the information then available suggested there was no need to worry about human health. It was written by a well-known blogger on nuclear energy who had paraphrased a private email written by a Massachusetts Institute of Technology (MIT) economist who had collected the data to make the case for calm in an email to a relative. It appeared on an online community called The Energy Collective (TEC), which carried ads and had a name-brand sponsor (Siemens) but otherwise controlled little beyond checking its posters' credentials and their command of the English language. The essay registered lots of hits, but as the situation at the nuclear plant deteriorated it was updated to be less optimistic, with new text posted both at TEC and at MIT's NSE Nuclear Information Hub. More views ensued, though one of the readers of the first post was himself a blogger and wrote about the TEC post at *Salon.com*, another online media site; he felt that the original essay evidenced such bias that it was evidently part of a pro-nuclear campaign, and that the community site's brand sponsor only confirmed this suspicion (Siemens makes parts for nuclear reactors, and its control systems in Iran were affected by the Stuxnet computer virus in 2010).

Salon somewhat resembles an old-fashioned media outlet in that it takes advertising money and pays a few people for their writing but otherwise aggregates stuff for which it takes no responsibility, the same way TEC does. So there was no recourse to standards for corrections or retractions; the only platform for clarifying the truth was with conversation between and among the two sites. Neither TEC's smackdown article on the piece nor the mostly obscenity-laden comments to the *Salon* post did much to set the record straight.

Yet the conversation yielded the truth, oddly enough. There was little to substantiate the *Salon* writer's conspiracy theories, and even less interest from readers in pondering them. Readers voted with their comments and eyeballs and it turns out that it didn't matter who was telling the truth. The conversation vetted the debate, somewhat unconsciously, and reduced it to a lowest common denominator: the truth was that the truth didn't matter, at least when it came to this row.

This conclusion was supported by the content that TEC, its sponsor Siemens, and *Salon* provided to the mediasphere. Corporate policies were (and are) posted for any to see, as were the bloggers' associations and past posts. Information on Siemens' nuclear-related products and services have been publicly available for years on its website. Thus the bloggers' assertions could be held accountable to the information available to the community, and to the opinions of other participants therein. What's interesting to us is that this vetting process occurred *about* the involved brands, not *with* them. TEC and Siemens couldn't convince anyone of their agnosticism any more than *Salon*'s blogger could claim righteousness (even though they tried). The conversation sorted things out for them. The truth didn't emerge from any specific point of view but rather from the interplay between the posts, comments, and communities.

The conclusion also stands in stark contrast to much of today's liturgy about the necessity of brands "publishing content" to promote their positions. In past eras, businesses took out ads to debate issues, like Herb Schmertz's major newspaper advertorials for his client Mobil. Otherwise, nobody in the enterprise tried to talk directly to consumers, unless it was through a sales brochure or answering the phone when it rang in customer service. Now, since the technology exists to link brands with consumers and their communities cheaply and immediately, nearly every brand does it, and there are two broad philosophies for getting it done. This case is an example of the belief that consumers arrive at truth through conversation, while the other belief is that brands should use technology to tell them truth directly (via brand-owned sites or other sources of content).

We don't think your content will be seen as "true" if you declare it, even in the context of contributing it to a conversation. You see, *brands can't talk,* if you think about it for a minute, because they don't exist the same way rocks or tax returns do. Brands are ideas and promises created by people who are speaking on behalf of the business operations that pay for their efforts. They're *lenses* through which facts are presented with a point of view—an opinion—so the stuff is biased by purpose and practice, which isn't a crime but certainly isn't synonymous with information, news, or the truth.

When you produce branded content—movies exclusively for YouTube, faux articles for your website, or musings by your execs about their vacations—there's nothing authentic about it, per se. It's paid placement, like the accusation the *Salon* blogger made against the TEC blogger. People talking for the brand. Owning a branded online community, in which you allow people to talk about your brand, adds more reasons for suspicion and disbelief because there's the lingering likelihood that biased people edit the content and nudge the direction of the conversations.

So is branded content an ongoing ad that doesn't admit it?

Conversely, open online communities are to truth what the Wild West was to justice. Everyone has a bias and ulterior motive, so there's really no need to worry about qualifications or intentions. You can assume that every participant starts with distrust and disbelief, and that they'll duke it out to reach takeaways that are lowest common denominators of depth and nuance. Whatever survives all that whittling will have had much of the bias scraped off of it, and thus get closer to the objective truth than not. Any junk you propagate into this mix with your brand attached won't contribute to these process-of-elimination conclusions and, worse, will relegate whatever you're saying to being just another voice. By definition, branded content transforms whatever truth you hope to communicate into just another opinion expressed by individuals working for your brand.

You can't control the conversation, and the more you put into it directly—whether intended to educate or entertain—reduces your brand position and believability versus strengthening it or communicating truth. It's up to others to do that through their expression and debate. Just because the technology exists to allow you to broadcast whatever you want to your customers doesn't mean that you should. You can't own the truth. Nobody can. It emerges (and changes) from the conversation. So consider these content development strategies:

Just because the technology exists to allow you to broadcast whatever you want to your customers doesn't mean that you should. You can't own the truth. Nobody can.

- **Make your brand a relentless source of factual data.** Instead of producing inane entertainment content, why not spend those resources on making better, deeper, and more frequent factually accurate information available to anybody who wants it? Since there's no way to ensure that bloggers or consumers will investigate things, or even have the capacity to discern truth, you could present it. Full stop. Be transparent on how you found it and why you're providing it.

- **Let people disagree.** Skip even the hint of spin, and that includes trying to get bloggers to get smarter or change their minds, whether behind the scenes or overtly by comments or counterposts. The mediasphere debate is about your brand, not with it, which means you need to learn to tolerate a ton of disagreement and misunderstanding (often purposeful). If you pay someone to promote your point of view, you will denigrate your message.

- **Actively encourage debate.** Instead of trying to own the content or the medium, spend your money supporting its independence. The logic of new media suggests that a greater number of conversations will yield a quicker route to conclusions. It also means that the more useless content you send into the cosmos the more your brand impedes this behavior. Until communities like TEC and sites like *Salon* embrace the institutional rules of the news media they've replaced (and we don't think that's likely soon, if ever), your best outlets for your brand won't have your brand name on them.

Ultimately, your business is not in the business of content publishing (except for the ways in which it always was, except that content was called "sales" or "company information," or a "marketing pitch"). Perhaps you should stick to publishing content about the products and services about which you're qualified to speak, and allow independent sites to separate the wheat from the chaff.

Post-reality TV and Collaborative Plot

So far we've focused on marketing successes, but sometimes there are great lessons and truths to be found in less successful enterprises. The following case is one of them.

We weren't more than ten minutes into our conversation with Simon Dickson, deputy head of documentaries at the United Kingdom's Channel 4, before we could so clearly see the connections between the man and his programs (Channel 4 is like America's PBS, only supported with advertising and required by law to take a broader programming mandate). Dickson grew up with a love of comics, especially those from the stable of Stan Lee's Marvel Comics. Lee specialized in ordinary teenagers who acquired superpowers, through such oddities as mutation (as in the case of the X-Men) or a spider bite, which is what causes mild-mannered Peter Parker to become Spider-Man. Dickson, in his day job as an adult, takes a somewhat similar approach to his subject matter, which means he usually points a lens at the lives of ordinary people that focuses and amplifies what is extraordinary and heroic (and sometimes villain-like) about them, taking what many would see as ordinary and showing it to be amazing (without need of a spider bite). He sees magnificence in the everyday and mundane.

Dickson's approach has been responsible for some notable documentary programming successes, such as *The Family*, which was filmed using twenty-one cameras to follow an ordinary family over the course of one hundred days. He described the show as "not a piece of reality TV. It's real TV. It's lovingly crafted." Another much-loved program was *One Born*

Every Minute, which was a riveting roller coaster of emotions set among the real people found in a maternity hospital.

But it is one of Dickson's less successful outputs that we've agreed to discuss; one that broke all of the rules of television and used the broadest possible range of social media and digital channels to achieve what he hoped would be an honest and true experience.

Seven Days, which ran in the fall of 2010, not only broke new ground in the documentary genre but was unlike any other program ever conceived on terrestrial television. Each program was made and broadcast in one week, made up of the last seven days of the characters' lives. As the marketing blurb noted, "A lot can happen in seven days."

It documented the lives of eighteen people living in the West London borough of Notting Hill, only it did so with the active participation of viewers offering advice and observations in real-time directly to the on-screen characters (through social media tools). So if a character was wondering about whether to date someone, the viewers could pitch in with their opinions, which would then be reflected by the character in the next show. The participants were shown dealing with their new celebrity status, reacting to comments from viewers meeting and interacting with each other for the first time on-screen. The viewers tweeted about the action on the show, then the on-screen participants tweeted back with reactions to the viewers' reactions to them.

Dickson had created something new, in which the real people in the show were not cut off from the real people who were viewing it. *Seven Days* not only let the real world in but incorporated it into the show's narrative. He dubbed this new genre "Porous Documentary TV."

The interaction from viewers right from the start of the program was bigger than expected, attracting more people to Channel 4's website on its first night than the hugely popular show *Big Brother* (which had been one of the mainstays of the schedule for a decade, though it had stopped running earlier that year). Audience ratings were disappointing thereafter, however, and declined from the million-strong number for the opening episode. According to its producer, Stephen Lambert, ". . . it didn't get the reception it deserved because the audience didn't understand it." He was immensely proud of it, but the marketing ". . . encouraged people to think . . . this was a successor to *Big Brother*, and people that would have been interested in it as a new kind of interactive documentary didn't come because they didn't realize that's what it was."

Others criticized the show for being set in Notting Hill—a region obviously made famous worldwide by the eponymous Hugh Grant–Julia Roberts movie—but regarded with suspicion by much of the rest of the United Kingdom. One reviewer, Nathan Bevan, writing at www.walesonline.co.uk, rather unkindly suggested that this was hardly a show about real people since his view of Notting Hill was a place where "you'll find the bookshop where Hugh Grant worked and more self-obsessed, middle-class Bohemian wannabes than you can shake a stick at—actually make that throw a stick at . . ."

This criticism is unfair and actually beside the point. The show covered a range of Londoners, all of whom were shown, warts and all. But the fascinating thing about the show was that this was not just reality TV but post-*reality* TV. Here was no "controlled experiment," where people were shown supposedly unaware of the public spotlight placed on their lives; no TV life in a Petri dish with viewers as inert spectators. The lines were blurred between creator and observer by the interaction facilitated as part of the way the show was conceived. The actors and viewers were fellow participants in cocreating the show's content, which was presented openly and honestly as the characters in Notting Hill got on with their lives. It wasn't fiction anymore. It was true.

Dickson's drive to reinvigorate documentary television continues. Like many innovators, he's convinced that it is better
to succeed or fail wildly than to create lukewarm, limited
successes. Shows like *Big Brother* or America's *Jersey Shore* are
changing what we expect from TV specifically and entertainment more broadly. Concurrently, generations are growing up
armed with social media tools and the expectation that they
have a right to be known by anyone, and to know everything
about everyone; the notions of six degrees of separation or
merely fifteen minutes of fame are out of date. These changes
require new processes to define what is true as well as how
it's spoken. It is a glorious ambition on Channel 4's part to
be one of the pioneers of television that is fit for a world that
is much smaller and more connected, and at the same time
much more chaotic and more complicated than it used to be.

The lines are blurring between entertainment and real life
all the time, and they challenge brands to find a way to define
and sustain their positions. While scripted drama and comedy
will still have a massive place in our entertainment schedules
going forward, we think that Dickson's experiment in Porous
Documentary TV suggests an interesting model for content
development. It shifts the interesting to the unmissable by
making a passive experience involving and creative. Channel
4's *Seven Days* took the conversation from the watercooler
into the show itself. It's a process of truth creation that other
media properties could copy and improve upon.

Social TV and Beyond

It is not easy to get into the BBC's sprawling offices at White
City in the outer reaches of West London. A complicated, even
Kafkaesque process involves protracted negotiations with a dis-
embodied voice at the initial security gate, then two separate
building passes get us to our trusty guide, Maureen Dearsley,

who is the assistant to Helen Normoyle, the BBC's director of marketing and audiences. Normoyle joins us a bit early and announces that she has only twenty minutes to chat. Lucky for us that those twenty minutes are informative and fascinating.

We went to the BBC to discuss its use of social media to enhance and to amplify its program brands. The BBC, along with other commercial channels, has embraced social tools to drive conversations around shows like *Have I Got News For You* (a satirical panel game), *Top Gear* (a show about cars), and TV's most successful global franchise, *Strictly Come Dancing* (known as *Dancing with the Stars* in America). Using social media like Twitter and Facebook to extend the reach and engagement with its program brands is already standard procedure.

"I am a big believer in truth in marketing," Normoyle says. "Organizations don't have a choice anymore." She continued to explain that we're still in the early days when it comes to understanding how social media impacts programming content and marketing, but that already it allows the BBC to connect with its target markets in new and more interactive ways. Audience feedback to the BBC's invitations to comment on shows, for instance, is reborn as material to be fed into the development of new programming. "People's innovation and creativity take things in new directions all the time," she explained, "so we need to recognize that we need to stay on top of this in real time for marketing, communications, and for research."

Perhaps this is why the decline in TV audiences as a result of social media, predicted by some pundits, has never materialized; in fact, the very opposite has proved to be the case. Shows that drive those watercooler moments the next day at work, like we described in the Channel 4 case history, are exactly the kind of content that people also want to talk about while the show is on air. The technological developments of the last five years have made this possible. But engagement isn't synonymous with truth. There's nothing inherently truthful in the processes of social media, but could the media suggest processes for how brands create content (for marketing in particular)? We brainstormed the idea with Normoyle, and we see at least five qualities:

- **Real-time.** There's something about content provided in real-time, in that its immediacy has a quality of truth to it that something more thoughtfully created might seem more artificial or contrived.

- **Speed and frequency.** When a commentator can post a thought and receive feedback almost instantaneously, there's a perception of truthfulness that decreases in direct relation to how long the exchanges take to complete.

- **Brevity.** We lose nuance and depth in short comments, but perhaps the feedback that the BBC receives has a unique kind of impact because it's reduced to the primary, most important thought the viewer felt needed to be communicated.

- **Extended.** The social exchanges that mirror some BBC programming involve people who have not had immediate experience of the shows being discussed, thus expanding the involved audiences. Does this type of larger audience yield more truth or less truth? Is there more or less truth in a primary experience of a show versus second any feedback or discussions on it?

- **Analog, too.** Social media proves to be not only a communications vehicle for truth but also a mechanism that allows the BBC to invent other ways for viewers to get at the core values of its programs. In regard to that final quality, Normoyle referenced the BBC's use of its own website and related social networks for *Strictly Come Dancing*. Through these platforms, it invited viewers who had unsuccessfully applied for oversubscribed show tickets to instead come to BBC Television Centre for a "*Strictly* experience."

Four hundred fans arrived on a crisp November day for a BBC *Strictly* tour, a unique *Strictly* show featuring past and present talent, and to learn a dance routine to be featured as part of BBC One's station identification logo. The special routine was choreographed by one of *Strictly*'s dance stars and performed in the central courtyard at the TV headquarters—the iconic doughnut. Material from the shoot was also featured on the show's website and Facebook page to ensure you could spot yourself in the action.

It's marketing content like that—not necessarily the magic of social media connections—that helps the BBC evolve to truly reflect and be inclusive of its audiences. The idea of "Social TV" requires that the BBC approach its content creation with that reality in mind.

"We are long past the days when people used to refer to the Internet as if it were one thing," Normoyle added as our conversation neared its twenty-minute mark. "It is crucial that we not make the mistake of thinking of social media as if it is one thing now. We need to stay focused not on what it does but how it allows us to connect with our audiences at every stage of their journey."

IS IT ALL A GAME?

Recent history has demonstrated that people love to play games. Farmville, Foursquare, Star.me, and other games on Facebook and other social platforms aren't simply addictive to many players but account for a significant percentage of

(continued on next page)

total traffic and activity at those sites. There's just something about the game experience that goes far beyond interactivity and engagement. What if we chose to call it *truth*? There's nothing to debate, question, or even consciously address when you play a game; no wonder about designer motives or biases, and no conflicting opinions about game structure. The moment-to-moment playing experience just *is* and, in that way, is utterly true.

The process of game play—the elements of the experience—could be applied to how you envision and deliver the experience of your brand, not conceived as an overt game but perhaps borrowing some of the qualities that make gaming so true. This is some far-out thinking, but it might be fun to consider:

- **Goals and payoffs.** What if your brand communications had deliverables beyond presentation of stories or ideas? Games always have a "something to do."
- **Context.** Games always occur within boundaries of concept and design. Does your marketing content consistently acknowledge the context(s) in which it's experienced?
- **Flow.** There's a reason why scenes in games occur, whether narratively and/or chronologically. Should your brand content reference past messages or events?
- **Winners and losers.** Though it might be anathema to traditional thinking, should your marketing processes allow some consumers to "advance" while others don't?

Conclusion

What if the core of your brand wasn't an idea or position but rather a *process*? What would make your brand true wouldn't necessarily be dependent on your content but rather on your mechanism of defining it. The brands that spoke most truly wouldn't possess the most truth; they'd possess an ability to tell truth clearly, creatively, and collaboratively.

Our research tells us that these "Three Cs" are one of the keys that smart businesses are using to unlock the value of brand truth:

1. **Clearly.** Any process involves a series of actions, whether mechanical, personal, or interpersonal, which means that every process runs the risk of abusing or even just subtly changing content. Clarity is vitally important on the front end of such behavior (along with its commensurate quality of simplicity). You could almost see an inverse ratio between the level of clarity and the difficulty in communicating it as truth; consider how hard it is to make declarations of nuanced improvements or incremental benefits, and how refreshingly empowering it is to be allowed to sell something that is obviously better than what the competition offers. The BBC shows aren't marketed as "a little funnier" than others. Disney doesn't sell theme park vacations that are "4 percent better than last year's." Brands that have instituted processes of truth default to clear, declarative brand messages that can stand up to the vetting process that sharing entails.

2. **Creatively.** It's much harder to tell the truth than it is to simply make things up from whole cloth. Truth isn't inherently sexy the way you can conceive an idea to be, and you have far fewer tools at your disposal to make it so (because you always risk going too far afield and making it untrue). Yet with this bigger challenge come the rewards of a truthful brand relationship with your consumers, so it's a challenge worthy of the creative talents in your marketing department and at your agency

partners. Think of Channel 4's approach to developing the creative content of *Seven Days* and how unwieldy it could have been, whether you consider it from a technical perspective (how to enable viewers to participate in real-time and make meaningful contributions, not just observe) or on the basis of plot (there's no reason to expect that a community of viewers could manage a story line that they'd want to watch). These are good challenges to embrace and we've seen numerous brands elevate their games to resolve them.

3. **Collaboratively.** This is perhaps the most profound of the Three Cs because it requires that you redefine the substance of your brand as the process itself and not necessarily a static idea or set of statements that you use processes to propagate into the world. Your audiences aren't just consumers any longer but also sometimes co-creators. It's the integrity and practices of the *connection* between these broad, diverse communities that define the truth of your brand, not how successful you are in filling it with what you want to see in it. Consider the TEC example in which its online communities are open terrain where ideas are shared with nothing less than wild abandon. (Okay, we're talking about business issues, so "wild" is relative.) Such online communities are models of the larger expanse of space available to your brand, not just through the Internet but in geographic, physical space, too. How you define the processes by which you engage with this new reality so that their outcomes will yield truth is far more important than what you initially think the truth should be.

Brands are still very much about perceptions and feelings and associations—these qualities make them true to your consumers, ultimately—but it's important that you focus on the mechanism of establishing and supporting them. Truth is an ongoing service, not a goal.

DELIVER REAL CHANGE CHECKLIST

1. Is there any part of your delivery that does not match the brand? Really? What can you do about it and which stakeholders do you need to recruit internally to change?

2. Do you deliver services that really differentiate your brand?

3. Are your consumers more comfortable than your employees with newer media channels? What steps do you need to take to get your employees up to speed?

4. Can you allow your consumers the space to publicly disagree with you?

5. Which three improved services can you commit to this year that will clearly show that you care as much about the consumer as you want them to care about you?

6. How often do you meet with your counterparts in operations (your level, in working sessions, not updates that have few to no consequences)?

7. If you had to use measures of action to judge the efficacy of your marketing versus awareness or other states of mind, what metrics would you use and why?

8. What percentage of your marketing communications is based on activities in which your business engages and/or delivers? If a majority of your content is based on promises of emotional or other associative benefits, what could you do to shift the emphasis to things you really do for customers?

9. Can you name the last time a brand in your category actually changed the way consumers learned about, purchased, or experienced a product or service? Was it your brand? If so, how did it come about and can you repeat it; if not, why not?

10. Sometimes affirming consistency represents change (instead of constantly swapping out rationales for why your customers should purchase your brand). What are you communicating now that strengthens what you promised or claimed in your last campaign?

3

Take Consumers on the
Brand Truth Journey
with You

"It was an incredibly innovative experiment," said
Adrian Hon, cofounder and CEO of Six to Start, a
company that creates transmedia stories, "but it was
a horrible book."

He was describing to us a novel called *A Million Penguins*
that Penguin Books introduced in 2007 as the first book
written by an online community. Over the span of only a few
months, more than seventy-five thousand people viewed the
site and nearly fifteen hundred registered to add or edit content for the novel (though two of them would account for 25
percent of the work). The result of the effort was a hodge-
podge of bad dialogue and implausible plot, and certainly
didn't qualify as worthy of reading for anyone but the most
stouthearted (or bored). But creating a readable book hadn't

been the purpose of *A Million Penguins*. Nobody who participated in the community was there because they had any intention of *reading* a book. Their priority was to *write* one, and in
this way the project was an unmitigated success.

Hon continued:

> Penguin has been setting trends in publishing since they
> came up with the paperback book, so they're used to experi-
> ments. They're also populists in that they want to empower
> readers to reach authors. So they reviewed the wikibook
> experience and revised their thinking, and then they were
> ready to try something different with digital. We Tell Stories
> was the result.

The brief for the We Tell Stories project was to make a good
story that could only be told online, so it would be native and
original to the Internet and not just an adaptation of a printed
book. This would involve working with authors to structure
storytelling in tandem with an ongoing set of actions: clicking,
scrolling, searching, and other behaviors that are unique to
the digital experience had to be not just integrated but readily
apparent as components of the stories that were as natural and
important as the authors' written text. Seven Penguin authors
volunteered to participate in the experiment *gratis*.

The stories were each unique experiments. The first, *The
21 Steps*, was a thriller set in London and tied into places ac-
cessed via Google Maps, which added not only interesting
visuals but also the elements of actual places and environments to the story experience. Readers would seamlessly
move among story text, geolocation, and imagery. The final
story was perhaps the most audacious, however. Entitled *The
(Former) General in his Labyrinth*, it was an adaptation of *1001
Arabian Nights*, only updated to present-day Pakistan and allowing readers to experience literally the labyrinth of confusion and pain that the story's protagonist described. You

navigated it, much like a map, with key twists and turns dictated by your choice or action.

"We Tell Stories let us explore a variety of formats for telling stories in a digital way, from interactive storytelling, branching narrative, and story as reward," Hon explained, "but the unifying idea was that the technology aspects should be hardwired into the creative content, if you'll excuse the pun. Digital wasn't just a platform for a story but part of the plot."

We see in this experiment the importance of prioritized intentions to communicating meaning, purpose, and, ultimately, truth. Interactive experiences like We Tell Stories provide an intriguing model for developing content of any sort; they define the substance of a story, brand position, or idea *with* behaviors instead of viewing actions as outcomes *of* said content. The messages in most marketing communications are intended for one purpose, namely, to be remembered. Retention is the desired outcome, followed closely by ongoing awareness and, at some future point, purchase. Content is defined as (hopefully) retention-worthy. Then some other stuff or actions are wrapped around it, raising it above the clutter. Humor is the most oft-used tool, but anything will do if it will help elevate or differentiate the message.

"Transmedia" is one of the terms used to describe the kind of work Hon's company does, and it involves using a variety of media (online or off) to tell stories. Central to the conception of content is that it must match the media channel in which it is delivered. It must make sense. Think of a video game by way of example: though a cinematic cut might display prerecorded video to fill in the plot, most moments in the game evidence clearly prioritized intentions. You find your character standing before a fork in the road, or an enemy stands before you with his sword drawn. As a player, you know what the game expects from you.

Now contrast that with a TV commercial or longer-form video on YouTube in which a creative idea is presented to you.

Rarely is there any structure to it other than the conventions of protagonist/conflict or setup/punch line. It's a *story*, after all, so anything could be (and is) inserted into such order and there's no way to determine if it's the most or least important. Games are a series of experiences of prioritized intentions supported by deep backstories, while most advertising is a rich story told through creative elements that conform to the experiences of a particular medium. Some of the most common interactive digital tools—such as friending, forwarding, or voting—are add-on behaviors in hopes of better packaging the message content.

But what if behavior were the content of the message? Could the truth and subsequent utility of messages be defined by what we ask someone to do other than simply remember them? Providing consumers with a clear, unassailably simple call to action could be the ultimate clutter-buster, useful on any media platform or through every channel. Prioritizing this content would be the way to define the approach. Like Hon's stories with Penguin, using an action either to make clear the substance of the communication and/or help define the use is the strategic opportunity. Prioritization requires clarity, not nuance. It's taking the risk of failing to communicate the totality of a brand position in exchange for making a direct connection on at least one action. Less asks consumers to think things about a brand and instead do one thing about it. This works because sometimes we equate simplicity with truth.

One truth is easier to communicate than many truths. It's as if a list of truths almost dares consumers to determine which is most important (or truest). And one of the main propositions of this book is that the alternate to truth isn't neutrality, or even partial truth. If something isn't true, it's either irrelevant (at best) or false (more likely).

Like truth overall, however, defining a single truth to communicate is easier said than done. It's hard to willingly sacrifice a potential connection on the basis of trying to guess the right one. Even some of the most targeted digital marketing still delivers a menu of brand benefits in hopes of capturing every potential sale, often under the guise of allowing the consumer to decide what he or she wants to know. No product or service does one thing, or can tell its consumers to do one thing, right? Well, we think there are many examples of companies that not only do just that but also reap the benefits from doing so.

Say it simply. Adjectives are often the enemy of truth.

The trick is coming up with different ways to choose and communicate one truth over the others, to prioritize your intentions as a brand, and ask for a moment of your consumers' time. You need to clearly signpost the consumer journey. We've researched at least six ways to do it:

1. **Tell stories with punch lines.** As with We Tell Stories, make a call to action an integral aspect of your story.

2. **Have a single use.** Apply the brand to one purpose and make it the sole focus of the message.

3. **Do one thing well.** Distill from all your brand benefits one functional benefit to highlight.

4. **Offer a clear improvement.** Discard enhancements or any other declarations of incremental improvement and make the case for something being boldly better.

5. **Fix something.** Right a wrong. Repair something that's broken. Make easy something that's hard.

6. **Say it simply.** Adjectives are often the enemy of truth.

Let's look at prioritizing intentions to signpost a simple consumer journey in detail.

Tell Stories with Punch Lines . . . Real Ones

Volkswagen sold all of two sedans in the United States in 1949. The company had been founded in Germany in the late 1930s to build a "people's car" priced within reach of industrial workers and farmers. World War II got in the way of it ever realizing its dream, but the postwar world seemed ready for an affordable German-engineered vehicle. Sales slowly climbed and, in 1960, VW hired U.S. ad agency Doyle Dane Bernbach (DDB) to create what would become an iconic series of ads for the VW sedan. "Lemon" read one headline under a large picture of the car, while the supporting text explained that the company's testing was so rigorous that it could make sure every sedan was of the highest quality. It sold consumer benefits, not brand promises, and the DDB work is still studied today for its brilliant combination of consumer insight and creativity. U.S. sales soared, aided in no small part by the vehicle's quirky design.

It was sometime also in the '60s that a game emerged in which you punched the person next to you in the arm when you saw a VW Beetle on the road. Like other travel word or observation games we've all played on long trips, and particularly similar to the "Yellow Car Game" played in the United Kingdom, "Punch Bug" or "Slug Bug" got players playfully slugging one another as they took turns looking for Beetles on the road. It has no known author or point of origin; it was simply something people learned about from one another and then shared further, and its organic nature spoke to consumer reaction to (and interest in) VW. It didn't hurt that Beetles, which weren't the name of the sedans but simply an informal reference, weren't terribly common on the road, as that would have made the game far too painful.

Fast-forward to 2010 and the brand is still primarily known just for the Beetle. However, VW manufactures multiple models and wants to establish its presence beyond its historic identity, while at the same time not losing its connection to its past. It also faces the challenge of crowded categories in each of the segments in which it competes. Sedans and SUVs tend to look somewhat similar, as no established brand would or should try to mass-produce a design as boldly different as the original Beetle, and that includes the other offerings from VW. You really have to look to see the differences, if only to find the badge and identify the manufacturer.

This challenge moved ad agency Deutsch, the car's new advertising company, to look to the 1960s for inspiration. But the team chose not to gravitate to the imagery or sounds of that decade. It would have been easy to recast the brand's heritage in some "if you loved us then, you'll definitely love us now" sort of menu-driven presentation of cars through the ages, etc., all to the accompaniment of classic rock songs. This would have been an obvious appeal to VW's middle-aged baby boomer consumer profile.

Instead, Deutsch revived Punch Bug, renaming the game "Punch Dub" and producing a series of traditional and new media elements that effectively delivered one simple, clear message above all others: look for VWs. For the viewers old enough to remember the original game, it was a brilliant call to action both of remembrance and present-day action, while it told younger would-be customers that there were a variety of VWs on the road. Whether anybody actually played the game was immaterial (though we're sure VW would be thrilled if it took on new growth organically). The "punch" of the punch line, so to speak, was simply true. There's no way to qualify or contest it. It didn't ask the viewer to believe, trust, or even understand an idea. The payoff was excruciatingly obvious and incontestable and, therefore, it seemed true.

The design of this campaign payoff helped deliver this brand truth by:

- **Skipping the backstory.** The settings, whether using actors or celebrities, were inconsequential. No backstory was required to engage with the substance of the presentations, no threshold of understanding that needed to be overcome other than grasping the immediacy of the circumstances (which were very simple). We'd bet that many of the people who saw the commercials or participated in any of the other media executions might not even remember the setups. This is a stark contrast to the many ads that we might remember for that every aspect, in lieu of what brands they presented.

- **Avoiding qualification.** Prioritizing the content of the campaign meant that there was one point to it, and the point wasn't a step toward (or otherwise tangentially attached to) a commercially relevant message. The creative execution didn't tell a joke or deliver a menu of ideas that viewers had to deconstruct, which would have given them ample opportunities not to believe or use one or more of the steps. At least in this example, the "punch line" really was nothing more than an actual punch.

- **Making no promises.** The Punch Dub campaign asks us to believe absolutely nothing. No promise of happiness, satisfaction, or even something as mundane as a better driving experience. There's no leap of faith required to grasp the message of the campaign: look for VWs. Viewers can choose to qualify that content with their own feelings—it's a great idea, dumb idea, or irrelevant one—but those qualifications come from them, not VW. Their reactions can and will be as "true" as VW's prompt.

Consumer reactions were also quite positive. The campaign ran for five months in 2010, yet VW sales volume went up 38 percent year over year (the industry overall was up only 19 percent). Weekly organic leads to the company's site increased almost 20 percent over the same period the year before. There was a 5 percent overall awareness lift for the full line of its vehicles in just over three months.

A simple case of action/reaction?

Have a Single Use, Like "Just Open the Box"

"They said all the right things, gave all the rational answers we'd expected," said Kari Axberg, corporate vice president for branding and advertising for New York Life Insurance Company, the largest mutual life insurer in the United States. She was describing the findings of consumer research the brand conducted in 2007, both focus groups and online, among current policyholders and people considering life insurance. "Only they didn't follow through. There were a hundred reasons to put off buying life insurance, but a fundamental cause was the difficulty we all have dealing with our own mortality. It's easier to buy a flat-screen TV or car, and it's also more immediately rewarding."

The research also revealed another interesting data point: consistency in consumer sentiment. "When we got to benefits and asked how people felt after purchasing life insurance, every interviewee told us that they felt they'd done the right thing, even if they wouldn't enjoy the benefits in their own lifetimes," Axberg explained. "This was the first time their answers were so consistent, and it suggested a very different approach to us."

The company's last campaign had focused on the obvious values and images of the New York Life brand: stability and reliability. Big New York skyscrapers and grand orchestral music spoke to the reasons why consumers could rely for their insurance needs on this huge, 162-year-old, Fortune 100 company. The TV commercials were literally shot from the outside looking *at* the brand, and its tone was very Wall Street, very formal, and very rational, too, which could be seen reflected in the opinions consumers held of the brand. They also were arguably good spots, and they presented many good reasons why consumers should and do buy insurance from New York Life. But the marketing wasn't consistently giving people enough motivation to act on their best intentions, and buying policies was (and is) the ultimate measure of whether consumers felt the positioning was true.

"We knew we needed to get to the benefits," Axberg noted, "and after some serious work with our agency, we developed a strategy around giving life insurance as a selfless gift. It was something you bought for yourself in order to give it to others."

This was a huge and potentially risky change in direction, since so much of the marketing in the insurance industry was based on education or on prompting the guilt of failing to buy appropriate insurance. New York Life itself had reflected both tendencies in its own ads based on the gift idea in the 1970s; the sketched illustration in one print ad portrayed proud parents visiting their children bearing a gift-wrapped insurance policy with the tag "happy anniversary" and the headline, "One of the few gifts designed to last a lifetime." The recipients, including a young grandchild, look on with that utter joy that was only possible to show in ads back when they didn't have to remotely resemble reality.

For the new approach to work, Axberg's team needed to find a way to recast the creative from an internal perspective—not an external look at the brand and its many benefits but a single, core emotional benefit that emanated from the inside, from the personal experience of purchase—and the tone needed to support that humanity.

"Our lightbulb moment was when the agency brought the gift box to us," Axberg recollected. "It was the same shape as our logo, [had the] same fonts, and [was] utterly simple. It worked on so many levels that you really didn't need to think about it too profoundly. I think that's what made the idea ring true. It's what our brand meant to consumers."

The idea of using a gift box as an icon was also somewhat edgy (remember, we're talking about insurance here), since much of the category was well into exploring spokeslizards, ducks, cavemen, a somewhat sonorous faux president, and a rather glib retail saleswomen. Various box treatments tried to do things with it, but none of the ideas came across as true to the simplicity of the message. The gift "aha" for Axberg's team needed to be a similarly immediate moment for consumers. The company opted for a simple box, and proceeded to launch the campaign in summer 2008 via print, radio, and online. The team noticed an uptick in awareness and purchase receptivity almost immediately.

And then the market tanked with the financial crisis.

Consumers became very suspicious of financial services products, and that was only after they'd recovered from the shock of having less money with which to avail themselves of such services. New York Life upped some of the rational components of its messaging but stuck with the overarching gift theme. It proved to be the right call. "Share of voice" continued to increase. Brand research was up, as was unaided awareness. Things have continued that way through the writing of this book.

"I think the truth of that single idea—the moment of gift-giving—brought a core element of the New York Life brand to the surface, and made it tangibly real," Axberg told us. "The qualities of humanity, connectedness, and trust between people, not just for our brand, have become the tonal mandate in all of our briefs. I'd rather get that one benefit right and inspire people to purchase than get a list of other brand attributes right but fail to be relevant and meaningful."

Offer Clear Improvement: Brother, Can You Spare an Internal Organ?

We have steered clear of behavioral economics in this book for two reasons. First, it's a hot topic that has been widely explored and written about elsewhere. Second, it has nothing to do with telling the truth. It is a way of repositioning ideas so that you believe in them more, but those ideas do not have to be innately true for this to be the case. For example, placing fruit at the checkout lines of school cafeterias in order to prompt more kids to buy these healthy foods does not teach us about how much students prefer fruit, or whether they understand its benefits better, or more truly. It is simply exploitation of convenience and of propinquity (i.e., they happily bought the junk food that was there prior).

Sometimes, however, repositioning things is all that is required to uncover the truth in them better.

One example of this is the phenomenon of mobile phone applications, or at least the more successful ones. If shopping for groceries in the United Kingdom via the Ocado app is easier and more simple than going to the website or indeed than getting in the car and trawling supermarket shelves in person, then Ocado has succeeded in delivering a brand truth: convenience—the essence of why people shop for groceries online in the first place. The brand is better served by repositioning shopping from the web onto the nearest smartphone.

We can see how this behavioral phenomenon devastated a prior business that had relied on similar prompts, such as newspaper classified ads (far easier to place, read, and share online) and printed phone books, such as the iconic *Yellow Pages*. In the United Kingdom, *Yellow Pages* is doing its best to stage some kind of recovery with a superfast, intelligent phone app for its online business, called Yell, that knows where you are and takes you to the service you require more easily than a mobile phone web search can (think listing, map, directions, and promotional info all wrapped up in a single behavioral prompt). Whether this attempt to revive the fortunes of the directory business will deliver or not remains to be seen, but the company's famous jingle, "Let your fingers do the walking," could be true and owned by them once again.

What's clear to us in these success and would-be success stories is that the behavioral prompt is best when it also enables access to a clearly obvious improved experience. You can be smarter about time and place, but content still matters, especially if you want to actually change long-term opinions as well as habits. So we cast about to find another example to illustrate this fact and arrived at an unlikely case: organ donation.

Talk about a tough subject for marketing, mostly because it's impossible for most consumers to even contemplate. (It makes buying life insurance seem like an easy step, doesn't it?) It's one of those topics that your rational brain tells you is completely appropriate to sign up for, but that your emotions insist you simply not think about it whatsoever. It is an area mired in controversy and misunderstanding. Religious strictures can play a part in some people's attitudes to organ donation. The proper business of organ donation is not helped by the specter of organ trafficking, which is the subject of scary fictional stories and of terrible news accounts around the world. Yet organ donation is an essential tool for restoring health, and the science (and people) behind it are truly wonderful.

About a third of UK adults overall have registered to donate their organs. Experts (and evidence, like waiting lists, deaths on the list, etc.) say that far more is needed. Some experts believe that achieving more registrations is not only in the population's best interest but that people would be more willing to donate if they grasped the relevance and value—the truth—of committing to donations. Some argue that making the conscious case for organ donation is a bridge too far and that there is the opportunity to use behavioral science tactics to deliver a step change. So, beginning in July 2011, drivers in the United Kingdom (excluding Northern Ireland) who apply for new licenses using the online application system are asked the question about donation, and for the first time it is mandatory to answer. (This has been common in some U.S. states for a number of years.) There are opinion formers who believe that the true step change is to make it an opt-out decision rather than an opt-in, but this remains highly controversial. Are people just that unable or unwilling to face the truth of taking a decision?

When the Scottish government wanted to increase sign-ups to the organ donation register in 2010, it and its media agency chose as a starting point the people who had gotten as far as visiting the website but had failed to sign up.

The Scottish government and its team took a different, functional approach, and asked whether the high number of dropouts was not because people's emotions overruled their logic but because there were just too many stages to go through before registration.

This approach resulted in a streamlined registration process that reduced registration costs by more than 15 percent. The techniques to improve the campaign included a mix of things. The media-buying agency did a set of cost-per-acquisition deals that significantly improved the efficiency of the buying as the Scottish government's limited above-the-line advertising budget was only spent when people registered, thus removing a high proportion of guess work. From then on, the client only paid for activity that worked, but this alone wouldn't have solved the problem. In a very simple move that is akin to shifting the position of the fruit in our behavioral economics reference at the start of this case, the team changed the mechanics of the advertisement to offer the registration form *within* the copy (not an extra set of steps). Taking the registration form to the user simplified the user journey so much that someone could opt to sign up as soon as he or she showed an interest in doing so.

When you know something is good for you and you have every intention of doing it, you still need it to be simple. Making desired actions simple can be quicker and better than making the actions we want people to sign up for desirable. In these instances, it's not about needing a bigger creative idea or better, smarter spin. There is no need for celebrity endorsement, and no requirement of a long-form film to prompt laughs or tears on YouTube. The content is the behavioral prompt, which means simplifying the journey allows those true actions to occur.

The Scottish government didn't make the case for organ donation; it simply made it easier to do it.

When you know something is good for you and you have every intention of doing it, you still need it to be simple. Making desired actions simple can be quicker and better than making the actions we want people to sign up for desirable.

Do One Thing Well: Fight Back When Food Slaps You

The spot begins with a few middle-aged guys standing around a smoking grill, sharing a typical tailgate moment. One character holds a plate of steaming chicken wings and is enjoying one of them, only as he raises it to his mouth to take another bite, the wing whacks him in the nose. He tries again and it slaps him again, much to the chagrin of one of his buddies. He refuses to give up and tries to outwit the wing, which slaps him every time as his friends look on incredulously. A car alarm goes off in the distance as our protagonist gives up, putting the wing back onto the plate, his face covered in red sauce and clearly upset. "Your favorite foods fighting you?" the voice-over asks, only to be answered by on-screen text reading "Fight Back Fast" and the image of a container of TUMS antacid tablets. The spot (dubbed "Food Fight") ends with our friend happily devouring his wings.

"We needed to make the message simple and straightforward," explained Rachel Ferdinando, vice president, GI Brands at GlaxoSmithKline Consumer Healthcare North America (GSK). "What made it powerful was that we externalized a real internal conflict." She and Ken Christensen, senior brand manager, TUMS, took us back to the simple truth that gave birth to the campaign six months earlier.

The TUMS brand had been around for eighty years, was recognized as America's number-one antacid, and had the highest brand awareness and association with heartburn relief in the entire stomach acid remedies category. But the last decade or so had not been kind to the brand. Competitors had emerged and claimed to provide benefits that GSK believed the TUMS brand owned and supported these claims with new technologies and aggressive advertising and promotions. The TUMS brand team responded with several years of inconsistent messaging and multiple new product launches that took time and money away from the base business. By 2008, sales were declining.

"In a sense, we'd lost our way," Ferdinando explained. "We'd become obsessed with what others were doing and not focused on what was authentically true about the brand. We needed to find our voice in a way that addressed the consumer right here, right now."

"We'd become obsessed with what others were doing and not focused on what was authentically true about the brand. We needed to find our voice in a way that addressed the consumer right here, right now."—Rachel Ferdinando, marketer for TUMS

Intriguingly, consumer research revealed that TUMS was the category leader on themes of safety, trust, and value. The research also identified a consumer need—fast heartburn relief—that not only was critically important but which no brand owned. "When we saw that, we literally said, 'Aha! We've found our single focus.' It's an unmet consumer need and it can be ours," Christensen said. The research also contained a qualitative comment that stuck with the team. "One consumer said something like, 'heartburn is like a lover's quarrel, since the food I love doesn't always love me back.'" The resulting creative brief focused single-mindedly on this insight and added a specific challenge for the newly hired agency, Grey: make TUMS stand for fast heartburn relief in an immediately interesting and engaging way.

"Our reaction was very visceral, like we could imagine someone smacking themselves on the side of their head," said Yin Rani, senior vice president and account director at Grey. "The client had reached a conclusion that was so focused on a single benefit, it was like the Holy Grail of creative briefs." In fact, the agency got to work before the details of the contract with TUMS were finalized, as the brand was in trouble and the agency couldn't hold back its enthusiasm.

The first meeting to review creative was in mid-September 2009, only two weeks into the formal relationship. Rani remembers the meeting:

> I remember going into the room with some trepidation since we had no safety ideas. The client wanted simple and direct, and our response was to take them at their word and give them only the creatively bold ones. Each treatment dimensionalized the idea that people had this internal conflict with some of the foods they loved, and had been qualitatively tested and had its own strengths and associations.

One of the executions, called "No Fear," was a campy horror movie take in which a scary food was revealed in a Hitchcock-like moment at which the TUMS product could offer the remedy to protect the consumer. Another one personified food as a character in a chase scene that could have been borrowed from an action movie, only when it catches up with the consumer, (his/her) TUMS antacid tablets effect the getaway.

But the third treatment, "Food Fight," is the one that stood out, primarily because it so powerfully externalized the inner dilemma of loving food that doesn't always love you back.

"Without that, the fast-acting message wouldn't connect," said GSK's Ferdinando. Consumers agreed, giving TUMS a greater than 10 percent bump in sales in 2010, and the momentum continued into 2011. "Food Fight" stands as the most successful and productive advertising campaign of any GSK brand in the United States (according to the company's internal media-effectiveness scoring) and prompted four new spots and a host of social media applications that are still bearing fruit.

We think the campaign worked because it so effectively prioritized the truth that TUMS wanted its consumers to associate with the brand, and did so through following three basic rules:

1. **Have a clear mandate.** The team at GSK was talking about truth long before it conceived the brand brief, and it made sure that it defined that truth in clear and simple terms. The team prioritized "fast-acting" internally, which gave GSK a guide to communicating the brand externally. The brand wasn't mandated to do a lot of things. It was directed to do *one* thing.

2. **Be creatively obvious.** While entertaining, the other creative executions on the brief warranted some deconstruction, whether understanding the faux movie references or associating foods with characters. The "Food Fight" campaign was brilliant because it required no such effort on the part of the viewer; the setups are all immediately obvious (i.e., somebody eating) and you immediately "get" the point.

3. **Un-nuanced payoff.** The TUMS spots are anything but nuanced, but the clarity of the creative is directly related to the benefit payoff. The humor also doesn't overpower the message but rather illustrates it, so when we see the happy consumer stuffing his or her face at the end of the spots, we also "get" that, too. The association between "indigestion" and "fast-acting" is obvious. For TUMS, truth was clear, obvious, and offered a fast-acting payoff.

Fix Something by Helping Customers Be Better Customers

There is one online community that has developed a strong, almost tribal sense of purpose over the last five years, perhaps more than any other, and grown in power, too. It is a community that was all too easy to dismiss in the past, but one now that politicians, nongovernmental organizations, and brands ignore or upset at their peril. It is fundamentally one to which you would be an idiot to lie—because no one should lie to his or her mother.

From small beginnings in the opening years of the twenty-first century, mom bloggers (or "mum" bloggers, for those of us in the United Kingdom) have found their voice. Moms' forums, such as *Mumsnet.com,* have grown in content (due to more moms blogging), influence, and traffic. It has been transformational for the power of moms who had previously never really banded together other than on a very local level at the school or nursery gate. Now mom bloggers are a scary force to be reckoned with for any brand attempting to sell them stuff.

Although it took them awhile to catch onto it, the Internet in general and social media in particular are ideally suited for busy moms. You can interact with your peers whenever you're awake (it's a great middle-of-the-night medium, should a mom be up with a baby in the wee hours), and you will always have one huge thing in common with your fellow bloggers/community members. Justine Roberts, who runs UK-based *Mumsnet.com,* has commented that she doesn't so much lead the community but rather serves as its puppet. There are a lot of very vocal and opinionated voices on the Internet that belong to mothers, and if you try to whitewash the facts of anything to them you're taking a big chance. Roberts gives the following advice/warning to advertisers about her community: "Get it right, and they'll tell the world. Get it wrong, and they'll tell the world."

Roberts gives the following advice/ warning to advertisers about her community: "Get it right, and they'll tell the world. Get it wrong, and they'll tell the world."

So, when in 2009 Tomy (makers of toys and nursery products) did an audit of how the online mom communities were feeling about the company, it was alarmed by what it found. Moms weren't feeling anything about Tomy at all. On the upside there was no negativity, but on the downside there was a good deal of silence, which rendered the pathway those consumers would need to travel—from unaware to knowledge, interest, trial, and purchase—long and expensive. This was particularly bad news for the team at Tomy because it had a new range of baby monitors to sell. So, based on the lack of online mom support, it decided not to.

Well, that is, Tomy didn't sell via the traditional route of advertising in magazines or on TV. Instead, the company came up with a completely new method of communicating with its audience. The baby monitor market had heated up in recent months, with a new set of competitors like BT introducing new technology. Tomy had traditionally led the market and its new range more than matched the competition. One approach could simply have been to specify the competitive advantages of Tomy's new technology, the traditional advertising solution being TV and parenting magazines. The media planner for Tomy, Nicola Jopling, was convinced that relying on traditional solutions was not good enough. Part of the reason for this was the company's recent research, but so was her own recent exposure to motherhood—not personally, but in the shape of her younger sister, who had just given birth. Keen to immerse herself in the new mother experience, Jopling had kept a close eye on how her sister had consumed media during the pregnancy and in the early days of motherhood. The first thing she observed was that her sister didn't read parenting magazines or watch any daytime television. So in this case, both of the main assumptions for this audience were incorrect.

Jopling took her research a stage further than simply watching what her sister did. She arranged to attend her sister's National Childbirth Trust group, which was a networking collection of moms who had taken antenatal classes together and then met regularly after giving birth in order to share experiences. Here, Jopling found that her qualitative insights about her sister rang true for the rest of the group, too. These regular moms spent the day out of the house at baby gyms, at coffee get-togethers, and in the park, leaving chores and media consumption to nighttime. They had a lot of buying power and a huge need for advice as they stepped into the great adventure of motherhood.

A great deal of their media consumption ended up being on parenting forums online. For many women it was the first time that they either sought advice online or offered advice and solutions. The early-adopter women who wrote and blogged online often did so with androgynous pseudonyms in order to deter the wrong kind of attention. Only once moms had found their power and their voice did gender neutrality cease to be an imperative.

Jopling made her case to Tomy and the team together decided that rather than compete in the territory of straight advertising around product specifications, it would get the moms online to start to talk about and with Tomy by asking them to share their top tips for parenting, whether or not Tomy had a product in that area. Tomy's strategy was to get moms talking about the brand by talking to and with them about motherhood.

Forty emails were sent out asking for the top mom bloggers', top tips. Team member Alexandra Gough remembers how nervous she was sending them out originally. She didn't want the women she was asking to help Tomy to take the request the wrong way. The answers were brilliant, and the team produced a booklet with "top tips for today's parents" instead of an advertisement for its monitor. All the bloggers were credited and their URLs were included, which also meant that the bloggers themselves were happy to promote the guide.

The online community's advice also led to a paper leaflet being produced for distribution at baby shows and retail outlets, as well as online content that was used to promote Tomy's product and overall reputation. Perhaps not so surprisingly, though completely organically, some of the top tips featured products in Tomy's range. But others, like the magical power of cotton wool and our personal top tip of the absolute necessity of having many, many muslin squares, related to products that are not made by Tomy. This meant that the offering had integrity, and the advice came across as truthful.

Sales of the Tomy monitors increased, but more importantly perhaps, the brand is now a regular contributor and enabler to the ongoing digital dialogue between moms. By shifting the focus of the activity away from product features and into the more interesting territory of advice for new moms, encouraging them to explore, embrace, and reach conclusions about the products that it knew were superior—letting them discover those attributes on their own terms—Tomy captured a position of strength and trust for the brand.

Say It Simply, and Just Let the Kids React

"Would you like a pony?" a businessman asks two kids as they sit on little chairs at a table that looks like they could be in a kindergarten classroom.

"Yeah," the first girl answers, and the man quickly pulls out a toy pony from his pocket and hands it to her. As she's beaming over her new toy the guy asks the second girl the same question. "Yeah," she says, nodding, only this time he calls a real pony into the room.

"Wow," the second girl says. The first girl is clearly disappointed. "You didn't say I could have a real one," she adds.

"You didn't ask," the guy answers, as if he's just told her she made a mistake. The little girl gives him a slow-burn look as the voice-over tells us it's wrong to hold out on somebody, and that Ally bank will notify you when your money could be earning more. The company's tagline appears: "Straightforward."

The campaign launched the Ally online bank brand, which was a component of a nearly hundred-year-old business that had grown by providing the loans for purchasers of General Motors vehicles. It had gone through many ups and downs, having recently gotten into the home loan business and required some of the U.S. government's bailout money. It had reorganized itself into a bank holding company and then, in 2009, introduced its online retail banking service. The campaign started with three spots that May, followed by others that each illustrated a banking experience by showing the viewer the same behavior in a context of how a kid would respond to being treated in such ways.

Perhaps not so surprisingly, it turns out that the kids hadn't been scripted. Their reactions were genuine. They'd been interviewed for their skills at communicating and comfort level with the environment, and then between ten and fifteen kids were shot so Ally's agency could choose the most convincing take. Kids reacting to simplified versions of the inanities that adult customers experience all the time—special deals that don't materialize, difficulty dealing with complicated menus when calling for service—with the same core emotions that all of us feel: surprise, disappointment, anger. Their reactions were true because they were real.

Now contrast that with any financial services or bank marketing you can remember. It's usually about promoting some vague promise—"we care" or permutations thereof—alternating with very explicit promotional offers of introductory rates or fleeting fee holidays. The sector, like many others, is consumed with menu-driven branding, offering consumers a lot of potential benefits, often without context, supported with declarations of trustworthiness. What Ally did was strip away all of the things it could have said about itself (you can

imagine what some of the unused creative proposals did with
its one-hundred-year history, responsibility for putting cars
into millions of people's garages, its vast size, etc.) and elevate
one fact above all others. It risked missing the opportunity to
promote a variety of truths about its brand to communicate
one in a believable and convincing way.

It helps that the company actually set out to deliver on
these benefits before choosing to promise them. In an earnings review from early February 2011, the company outlined
its "Differentiate the Customer Experience" strategy:

- Access to customer representatives 24/7.
- Ease of use—streamlined account opening process, easy
  navigation on website.
- No hidden fees, rules, or penalties.

The path from each of these efforts to one or more of the
advertising spots is bluntly obvious. Ally was promoting what
it preached, and each benefit stood on its own as a simple customer truth. The company spent north of $95 million in 2009
to deliver this select information to its would-be customers.

Not everyone loved it. Some marketing reviewers saw the
immediacy and truth of the spots, but others felt that negative approach was too contradictory to the precepts of proper
branding, which dictate that you don't knock your own industry by claiming you're somehow different. Even if the
points raised were each absolutely and utterly true, the brand
should have focused on the positives, they said, even broadly,
instead of selecting individual points to address, whether positively or negatively. The use of children was also questioned,
as the blogosphere was full of comments from consumers
who objected to how the children were treated, likening it to
child abuse since the disappointment on the kids' faces was
so real as to seem purposefully painful to them. Comments
from folks in the banking trade felt that it was disingenuous

for a bailout-taking brand to promote much of anything to the outside world.

To us, this was evidence that truth hurts sometimes. These were all reasonable reactions to the truth inherent in the Ally spots. Bad treatment is bad, however it might be explained away or otherwise ignored. We take the negative reactions as a positive. And consumers seemed to have few problems with it, choosing instead to respond to the truthfulness of the message with their money. Ally's retail deposits went up for six straight quarters during the campaign. In July 2010, more than 90 percent of its customers reported that they were "satisfied" or "extremely satisfied" with the bank, and just under 90 percent said they'd recommend it to a friend or family member. This only further affirmed the truth of its branding. *Money* magazine named it the "Best Savings Account" in 2010.

The brand truth of its offer was illustrated by the truth of the alternative: getting treated well versus being treated poorly.

PLAY THE INTENTIONS GAME

The viral video is hilarious. Somebody gets splashed in the face. A girl's top falls off, or a guy's hair catches on fire. Maybe somebody just talks funny, or makes a joke about her car, MP3 player, or hair color. Same goes for TV commercials or magazine print ads. Bold pictures. Colors. Jarring designs and goofy narratives. We see them all the time.

Often we can't remember what brand paid for the privilege of entertaining us. So we say let's make it into a game, which we call "Intentions." Here's how it works:

- You need two or more people to play.

(continued on next page)

(continued from previous page)

- Click on a video someone has sent to you, or pay attention as a commercial starts.
- Yell out what you think the industry type and/or specific brand name the content is selling.
- Floor polish! Insurance! ED medication! Boat rentals! Anything goes, but you're trying to get it right.
- Once the spot ends, tally your score based on the following values:
  - one point for guessing the right industry type
  - two points for guessing the right brand name
  - one point for guessing the wrong brand name in the right industry category

There's an alternate version of the game in which you use a timer and weigh quicker answers higher than slower ones, but it gets a bit complicated and most of the spots you'll end up watching are pretty short anyway.

Once you start playing "Intentions," you'll see just how hard it is for much of what we see on TV or online to seem true at all.

Conclusion

For a generation suffering from information overload and a resulting confusion and sense of unease, prioritizing intentions is a fancy way of saying, "Tell me what you want right up front so I can understand it." Its truth is a truth that is desperately needed, perhaps even more so because while properly doing so is difficult, prioritizing intentions happens all the time. Much of what we see with new media, especially campaigns intended to be virally social, is very much focused on one intention: get the viewer to laugh, with a secondary intention of warranting a pass-on. Jokes require setup and a dramatically effective delivery, and they presume that the viewer will "get" the humor. The same goes for the intention of much branding overall, which assumes that consumers will remember something otherwise unattached to a brand because it was presented creatively to be attached and then, sometime on another day, remember to attach it to another intention, like the intent to recommend or buy something. There are any number of qualities in such communication that can be challenged, debated, or disregarded altogether. No brand can own "funny." So it's hard for it to be qualified as true.

> *For a generation suffering from information overload and a resulting confusion and sense of unease, prioritizing intentions is a fancy way of saying, "Tell me what you want right up front so I can understand it."*

Some brands have avoided the prioritized intentions challenge completely by outsourcing marketing content to users (user-generated content is also called UGC). Consumer priorities come first, whatever they are, because they will be more truthful than anything brands can produce. Instead, businesses should "curate" this content. Yet there's nothing definitionally truthful about UGC, especially considering it originates based in large part on what brands have previously communicated. Rather, it's just not obviously dishonest or suspected of ulterior commercial motives like the *subsequent* content coming from brands. So measures of views and clicks speak to its format but not necessarily its utility, let alone truth. We could consider it content that consumers create in spite of brands, not for or because of them, or because it's particularly true.

Do consumers know the objective truth? Of course not. It feels good to say it but it's just not true. What they know is true to them, but how they arrive at it comes from some endlessly reflective hall of mirrors that incessantly plays and amplifies what they say and think back to them. We think brands have the obligation not only to have input into this process (as participants) but to prioritize their intentions in doing so (in other words, be clear and show some leadership). Communicating truth should be the top priority, bar any other purpose. Making it memorable and sharable are tactical concerns, not strategies.

Communicating truth should be the top priority, bar any other purpose. Making it memorable and sharable are tactical concerns, not strategies.

In this chapter, we shared six ways to prioritize truth, all of which helped deliver sales and awareness, and did so far more than what we could have expected from merely smart or targeted marketing. Our research yielded many more examples, but to summarize the takeaways we'd say there are three broad elements to how prioritizing intentions can help your brand be true:

1. **Focus your campaign on a single brand truth.** The days of nuance are over. There must be a declarative fact about your brand that you know (or believe) matters most to your customers. If you don't have one, your problem is far bigger than anything marketing can fix.

There may be dozens of things the world should know and appreciate about your brand, but a fifteen-second or longer spot or online video get old equally fast. You really have only a few seconds to tell people something that might matter to them. Prioritize what you want to say and then delete everything after the first point.

2. **Make it tangibly real, not a reference or allusion.** To say it again, the days of nuance are over, and your consumers' starting point is going to be suspicion and disbelief for anything you choose to share with them. So the structure of your communication, irrespective of format, should be designed to substantiate your truth. Be creatively insane, funny, or overcome with pathos, but do so with the sole purpose of dimensionalizing your single brand truth. Ruthlessly focus on your truth and don't let your execution get distracted by a great joke or otherwise wonderful idea. You have a short time to prove something. Do it, don't just say it.

3. **Prioritize your expectations by what gets you closest to sales.** The argument that your consumer wants to absorb some form of content without any utility for a purchase transaction is not new; branding advocates were promoting the same idea in the 1960s in support of TV commercials that had no closing pitch. Making sure you have some motivator for purchase behavior in whatever you produce—again, be it a print ad or viral video—is quite distant from making it a hard sell. There's a broad range of ideas you can rely upon to make it clear to your consumer that you have a purpose beyond being their friend and that you're willing to be transparent about it. After all, telling the truth means telling the truth.

4. **Finally, consider why you bought this book.** We wrote it because we wanted to give you a new way of looking at

your business, branding, and marketing practices, and to give you immediately actionable ideas for trying out new things. We suspect that you bought the book for the very same reasons. Our intentions not only were prioritized similarly but they were in many ways identical. There is something inherently true in such a meeting not only of minds but of purposes, isn't there?

CONSUMER JOURNEY CHECKLIST

1. Have you given the consumer an obvious way to participate in your brand in some way? (Pack design, flavor creation, or advertising slogan for them to repeat?)

2. Can you create a community of fans around your brand that is more than a social media site? What could you talk about other than marketing creative?

3. Can you simplify the purchase journey? Could your brand own this truth?

4. If you took your logo out of your ad, could you easily replace it with one of your competitors'? If so, what can you do to stop this from ever happening again?

5. Can giving advice about products that your customers need but that you don't sell or make give your own brand claims credibility?

6. When was the last time your brand admitted that it didn't know something or that it could use customers' help to improve things? How did you communicate it, and how did your consumers react?

7. What are the three topics you know your consumers want to talk about (or talk about among themselves) that your brand doesn't want to address? If you can identify

them, why aren't you figuring out ways to participate in those dialogues?

8. If you could say only one thing about your brand—ever—what would it be, and why? If it wouldn't be enough to prompt consumer purchase, what could you come up with that would work instead?

9. If you created a ratio of entertaining content versus information that presents truth(s) about your brand or motivates purchase in any given social media conversation or ad, what would it be? If the ratio is weighted toward entertainment, how could you shift your content toward truth?

10. Answer quickly: What's the one reason why your category would suffer if your brand didn't exist? Why would consumers miss it?

4

Enlist Third-Party
Advocates

"**W**iki" means "quick" in Hawaiian, and Ward
Cunningham meant "really quick" when he in-
stalled WikiWikiWeb on the Internet in 1995.
An online wiki meant ease of use via a browser, quick and in-
tuitive linking between topics, and a spot that visitors couldn't
just experience casually but that actively encouraged their
participation in the site's content and appearance. Now the
world has wikis for everything, from the encyclopedic breadth
of Wikipedia to the revealed secret minutiae of WikiLeaks.
Most governments, nongovernmental organizations, and
businesses have online forums for user-accessed information;
these, too, are wiki-*fied* to varying degrees.

Your brand is a wiki. Truth is a wiki, too. Consider these
ideas for a moment.

You're probably aware of the participatory nature of your marketing these days. Online marketing campaigns let your consumers or customers watch multimedia content, perhaps share it, and sometimes download, change, and repost it back to your brand. Contests allow people to create ads for your products and earn charity dollars or pounds for their favorite causes. Facebook pages let people "friend" your brand, and it's likely there are tweets both from thrilled and dissatisfied customers swirling around in the ether. When we talk about interactive, digital, or social marketing, it's these sorts of activities that we believe define the new, collaborative nature of our audiences' participation with our brands. The mechanisms of new media technology require that we address it in the delivery of our marketing.

Our research found that the *outcomes* matter far more than the mechanisms of interactivity. After all, collaboration on marketing still yields marketing; it's engaging with an audience on content that they well know is intended to get them to do something or other, so the number of participants speaks to the reach of the marketing but not necessarily the substance of it. It's no surprise that the emerging trends on social media metrics are to look for numbers on tests, purchases, and other real-world behaviors that resemble the actions marketers have long sought to prompt. It's also a general truism that if marketing content is the primary purpose of engagement, the product of such collaboration is often derivative of content that was created by people who know what they're doing. The "crowd" tends to give back what it has been given (or shown). So, it's only a start and it may not get them appreciably closer to doing things that matter to them or to your brand.

What does get them there? How do consumers form an understanding of the truth about brands that matters to them? We think that process looks a lot like a wiki, and that it happens beyond online interaction, at another level altogether— a higher level or "meta" level beyond the reach of marketing exclusively—where the content of not just your marketing but the outcomes of your staff interactions, news announcements (and those of your critics), analyst reports, and all of the other business activities are traded, compiled, and assessed by your employees, vendors, customers, and critics. This is the *content* of your brand and, as such, it adds up to a running narrative of its truth.

This means it's not enough to have a conversation with these various groupings or classes of people. The mechanisms of conversation don't necessarily have any inherent value (though more on that later). Your conversations must yield *truths* that are believable, supported, sharable, and motivational. The content of your conversations matters most, and that means your audiences' involvement needs to be focused not on creating marketing but on developing truth.

Your conversations must yield truths *that are believable, supported, sharable, and motivational.*

Think about channels and audiences that need to be engaged, but whether or not they influence, promote, or commit their firstborn children to the service of your brand is but a tangential outcome to their involvement. They must first and foremost help you define the truth. They are not so much cocreator consumers of your content as they are interest group codefiners. The starting point is to enlist others into your brand. We see five ways to get at elements of your brand truth, and each involves engaging with a different perspective, ranging from affirming your position through the actions of sympathetic individuals through to means testing your brand truth with distrusting or doubtful communities.

These five target markets to enlist are:

1. Employees
2. Cynics
3. Advocates
4. Critics
5. Agnostics

Let's explore in detail how each type of relationship can be used to create brand truth.

Employees: Co-owning Customer Experience

The extraordinary story of upmarket UK department store chain John Lewis dates back to the son of the founder of the first store on Oxford Street. Born in 1885, John Spedan Lewis was the eldest of two boys. By the age of twenty-one he'd been given a quarter-share holding in the store. He became aware that he, his brother, and his father among them earned more than the entire workforce put together (his father was also known as an autocratic leader, which wasn't uncommon in those days). When a riding accident forced him into a long convalescence, Lewis had a vision for the company that created a different model for the relationship between employer and employee that focused on fair treatment.

Lewis's father didn't exactly approve of all of his ideas, and it was only after his death in 1928 that Lewis assumed leadership of the company and had the authority to put his radical thinking into practice. He formed the John Lewis Partnership, which made every full-time employee a "partner" and gave him or her a share of the company's profits. Eventually "The Founder" (as he came to be known) signed an irrevocable trust settlement in 1950, which meant that the partnership became the property of the people employed within it.

Today, there are two things that most everyone in the
United Kingdom knows about John Lewis. One is its long-
standing marketing slogan (unchanged since 1925), "Never
knowingly undersold" (this promise is somewhat complicated
by Internet shopping). The other is that John Lewis is not
staffed by employees but by partners. Not only does every employee share in the profits, but he or she can also influence
company policy through company surveys and a set of coun-
cils and committees that feed the partners' opinions back to
their main democratic body, the Partnership Council. Each
store has a branch forum selected by partners to represent
them. Freedom of speech is "guaranteed."

Although it has never been marketed as a brand benefit,
the point of difference in ownership is tangible when you visit
a branch of John Lewis. It's not that every experience you have
as a customer is fabulous; John Lewis can be as unsatisfying as
any other busy shop on a crowded Saturday afternoon, particularly when there are sales under way. But it is patently obvious that the partners take pride in their work and that they
are empowered to have an opinion and to act on their own
intelligence and experience. The individual serving you may
be superb or he or she may be frankly average. The company
certainly doesn't have a monopoly on genius sales associates
who know exactly what you should buy your cousin for her fif-
tieth birthday. The individual serving you might frankly even
be quite grumpy on occasion. But they don't come across as
bright and shiny, well-trained automatons, and they are never
ever uncaring or indifferent. They also pride themselves in
maintaining relationships with customers who return again
and again.

We are living proof that this policy works. Like most English people, Sue has been going to John Lewis stores all her
life. Sue remembers going as a child with her mum to buy a
boring school uniform and then wondering excitedly about
the chance that they would also drift into the toy department.

She'd return again and again when she was pregnant with her first child, visiting their excellent maternity department to spend a fortune (or so it seemed), and then repeatedly as John Lewis became for her (as it had with her mother) the default premium choice for household items, gifts, and things for her young family nesting in the London suburbs.

A 2010 TV advertising campaign for the store summed this up by showing the life span of a woman shopper from birth to old age, accompanied by the song "Always a Woman." The ad itself was somewhat polarizing, as it tended to both sentimentality and stereotyping; however, it succeeded in creating its own "watercooler moments" among the chattering classes, with general consensus that only John Lewis could have got away with it. As journalist Libby Brooks wrote for *The Guardian* online in April of that year, ". . . because it's John Lewis, a company so nationally adored that a recent docusoap about its management topped the ratings, cynicism must be set aside. . . ."

The John Lewis brand does not straightforwardly claim to be employee-focused. It couldn't, really, as such declarations are too commonly made and rarely substantiated. It more directly demonstrates it in every part of the experience for its customers because of its internal relationship with its sales team, who are all partners. This goes beyond the exigencies of employee morale-building campaigns or even financial reward schemes and engages with its partners to quite literally codeliver the business. In doing so, the partners collaborate on creating the truth of the brand. As they say themselves, "The John Spedan Lewis way is as alive today as it was eighty years ago."

This truth should be seen as a direct contributor to the brand's success. John Lewis is one of the United Kingdom's top private companies, with consistent profitability and bonuses for the partners. In addition, the John Lewis Partnership has a very extensive program of social activities for the partners, including two large country estates with parklands, playing fields, and tennis courts; a golf club; a sailing club with five cruising yachts; and two country hotels.

Cynics: Questions and Answers

The first episode in Ford's *Bold Moves: The Future of Ford* documentary series starts out as a very-well done but standard corporate propaganda piece. You see images of the past interspersed with seemingly unscripted snippets of employees talking about the company's heritage. Then, about ninety seconds into it, a journalist says that the American auto industry is in a state of crisis and that Ford "is really a company that could go down." A newspaper headline declares how much the company lost in a single quarter, and then somebody talking at a dealer meeting says, "Our pricing is totally irrational." Customers complain on camera. Ford employees talk about failures and plant closings. "Change or die, baby. That's what it's all about," Chief Marketing Officer Mark Fields says. Then the clip ends.

It turns out it wasn't standard-issue propaganda after all.

The year 2006 seems like distant history (or a different planet). It was certainly a different time for the American auto industry. Ford, just like its Detroit competitors, was suffering what could be charitably called a crisis of confidence. Nobody believed that Ford had a clue about what was going on, and therefore not many people believed much of what Ford had to say on the matter. A cover of *Time* magazine in January of that year was both telling and biting: over a picture of Bill Ford the headline read, "Would You Buy a New Car from This Man?"

"The conversation was so loud and negative that it wasn't just overriding the positive stuff but also the facts," explained Beth Waxman-Arteta, president of client services at JWT New

York, and one of the creators of the "Bold Moves" campaign. "We knew we couldn't promote our POV in ads, and Mark believed in the people and the work under way in the company, so we decided to bring the conversation inside."

What that meant was hiring filmmakers to create content by talking to Ford lovers and haters, and then giving them unfettered access to Ford meetings, events, and people to discover what was going on. The footage would get chopped into five-minute episodes and released based on topics that were trending online, enabling Ford to substantively lead conversations, not just offer up its position. One of the early episodes included a critic who believed that Ford vehicles had "the worst mileage of anybody"—which directly challenged Bill Ford's avowed vision—so the video crew poked around internally and discovered the suspicion was unfounded.

"They got thrown out of a couple of meetings," Waxman-Arteta remembered, "and while the folks at the top bought into the concept, it was hard for some people who were doing the day-to-day work to deal with these cameras in their faces. They had no experience having to explain themselves as the video rolled, and it wasn't necessarily comfortable." The campaign sometimes included cameras trained on the filmmakers who were investigating the stories, in part to add another dimension of reality to the shooting, but also to let the Ford folks know that nobody was outside the view of the lens.

Ford's "Bold Moves" campaign ran for about a year and included more than forty films, a weekly refresh on a specially themed website, and an editorial presenting "for" and "against" points of view on the issues being explored within the company. Many influential industry bloggers reacted positively to this level of candor and often reposted the content verbatim. Sentiment started to change as critics were satisfied by some of Ford's actions and became advocates for the company's success, while still maintaining their independent credibility. They didn't like everything they heard, and Ford made a conscious decision to respect those opinions. Overall perception metrics went up, and there was evidence that consumers who visited the Ford Bold Moves website prior to visiting the Ford website were more likely to purchase.

Sentiment started to change as critics were satisfied by some of Ford's actions and became advocates for the company's success, while still maintaining their independent credibility. They didn't like everything they heard, and Ford made a conscious decision to respect those opinions.

The clips weren't commercials and they weren't promotional content in any traditional sense of the term. JWT calls it brand journalism. "It's PR meets advertising meets the truth," Waxman-Arteta added.

We think the approach fundamentally challenges and then creatively addresses some of the presumptions about conversation and its relationship to the truth.

- **Ford did nothing new to address the concerns of its cynics.** It didn't hatch a program to respond to concerns of one interested audience or another, and it didn't turn to a marketing campaign to try and reach out to them and change their minds. Ford effectively flipped the funnel and brought the attention inside to its ongoing activities. This approach was far more truthful than anything else it could have done.

- **It solicited the involvement of an impartial third party.** The invitation of impartial journalists to document its efforts gave Ford the credibility that it couldn't earn on its own. However unfair, this was a fact, and it was a really smart move to acknowledge this reality and act upon it. Think of all the time it saved avoiding trying to qualify or analyze the concerns of its cynics, and instead choosing to focus on what it was doing proactively to build the company.

- **It included questions with its answers.** For brands that have engaged in ongoing conversation with various critics, you know that those debates have a tendency to 1) never end and 2) leave your most die-hard critics still critical of your business. Brand journalism isn't the answer or the only tool for changing this dynamic, but we're intrigued by how it took Ford out of the position of being reactive and allowed it to challenge itself, pose questions, and include them as an integral part of their answers. This allowed the brand to take a leadership role in its conversations.

Ford enlisted its critics and their questions into a conversation that yielded truths that could be difficult for either side to stomach. Vocal critics couldn't deny facts that were reported to them, even if they risked losing some of the force of their arguments. Ford employees would tell the camera that their efforts were a work in progress, and that there was a lot left to be done, which sometimes required uncomfortable transparency. But it was the truth of the brand.

Advocates: More Than a Promotional Event

When Corin Dimopoulos, director of cycling, sports, and news for Sky sat down in the cafeteria at Sky's buildings in Isleworth on the outskirts of London to meet with us, he ordered a full breakfast, bought strong coffee for all, and then said, "For the last few years, it's been my life," referring to his work at Sky, specifically "Sky Ride," an ambitious campaign to get Britain cycling.

This is the guy who filled London with bicycles in lieu of cars and buses for the 2010 Sky Ride event, held in cities throughout the United Kingdom. It's now an annual festival of cycling that promises to touch more cities and keep more combustion-fueled vehicles in their garages in the years to come. Each event involves covering the roads in banners for its brand in what you might initially think is a fairly typical corporate promotion. It's anything but, starting with why on earth would Sky worry about getting people on a bicycle, and what truth does it communicate to the world?

Sky is the largest pay TV broadcaster in the United Kingdom, with more than ten million subscribers; it has been challenging its competitors in TV broadcasting and services over the last decade. Its main business is providing broadcasting services, broadband, and content for its customers. A recent check revealed no offers of bicycles or related equipment for sale.

Yet the thinking within Sky three years ago was that it could engage in an activity unrelated to its core business—a project with an intention having more to do with driving advocacy of the brand than it did with selling brand benefits (or writing subscription contracts for its services). It's this thinking, along with lots of hard work, that mushroomed into a partnership with one of the United Kingdom's most successful, if less immediately obvious sports.

If you asked most people outside the United Kingdom to pick the most typically British sport, they would start with one out of the following three candidates: cricket, soccer, or rugby. Recently, however, cycling has grown from a niche activity into one of the sports of which the British are most proud. You can blame a guy named Chris Hoy for this. Hoy's personal record is astonishing—four-time Olympic champion and ten-time world champion—and he helped make the Beijing Olympics a transforming moment for the sport, as the cycling team brought back eight gold medals. Interest in the sport has grown commensurately; much of the excitement about the 2012 London Olympics has frequently centered on Britain's cycling hopes. It isn't a coincidence that the very first completed venue was the fabulously space age–looking (or Pringle, according to some) new Velodrome.

Enter Sky. It has an ongoing corporate responsibility program that it takes seriously, and the team noticed the increased interest in cycling as a sport. It would have been simple to allocate funds to sponsor a team or race, or perhaps fund a children's program. That would have been standard branding strategy, and doing something worthy and then talking about it in marketing materials would have been very appropriate. Dimopoulos and his team got it in their heads that Sky could do something more, something truer to its customers and the public at large.

Its ambition was at once simple and utterly huge: find a way to get more families in Britain on bicycles and, in the process, create advocates for Sky in the saddle. Its strategy wasn't to put its brand signage in front of consumers (though it did that) but to focus on getting them participating in the sport.

This is when Dimopoulos takes a long swig of coffee, because the Sky team set off down a path that would take many months of intensive and sometimes unprecedented effort. It started with a question: how could Sky help the United Kingdom stop just *watching* the sport—an obsessive national pastime, particularly for those dominated by the Y chromosome—and get more people, X and Y alike, to *participate* in it? Therefore, the first task was to identify the sport that people would be most likely willing to join. Generally speaking, enthusiasm for participating in the most iconic sports for the

United Kingdom—cricket, soccer, and rugby—is naturally high and encouraged by schools, encouraged by corporate sponsors, and doesn't need more promotion. It is also predominantly male (with certain exceptions). Dimopoulos wanted a sport that could make a difference to whole families, not just boys or men.

His rigorous research dimensionalized the cycling opportunity. In addition to its rising popularity, cycling at the time was relatively naked of brand associations compared to soccer or rugby. It was a sport that Britain was good at in many different profiles—senior, junior, men, women, able, disabled, track, road, BMX, and mountain biking. A cross-agency multidisciplinary team was put together just before the Beijing Olympics in 2008, led by Dimopoulos and dedicated to getting one million more people in Britain cycling by 2013.

There were lots and lots of ideas generated. But the strongest (if not the easiest) one was the idea of shutting down city centers for the day in order to encourage thousands of families to come and cycle around the trafficless city. The truth of staging such an event would be inescapable.

The challenges of shutting Britain's busiest cities to traffic for the day and turning them into playgrounds for families were inescapable, too. They were also very motivating, almost reckless in their audacity. Dimopoulos was not only up for it but almost savored the dare, as did his entire team (they were told internally that succeeding wildly was the aim, and that they should strive to fail miserably rather than produce something that was just okay). He asserts with great conviction that if everyone who was indifferent to cycling would come to a Sky Ride in a major city, then they'd convert to being cycling advocates (and Sky advocates) on the spot. And that's not bluster: the experience of seeing London without cars and buses, but thronged by families on bikes, is mind-blowing and transformative, as if any individual has the chance to follow in Chris Hoy's pedal straps and accomplish anything to which they set their mind.

Months and years later, the campaign is on its way to becoming an institution as it tracks well against its ambition to get more Britons cycling regularly. There were five cities involved in 2009, ten involved in 2010, and fourteen in 2011. Hundreds of thousands of people participated. The advertising activity for Sky Ride is very local, focusing on citywide posters, local radio and press, regional digital, and PR activity. The intention of the advertising is purely to get people to come out and ride, not to show off about corporate responsibility at work.

You need to go no further than meeting with the Sky team responsible for Sky Ride to grasp the truth of this endeavor. The team's excitement around the next phase of the campaign is tangible. Rarely do they talk the language of branding—messaging, positioning, or the intricacies of brand extension and awareness—but they do speak about getting people to ride bikes. Incessantly, actually. And this is at the core of Sky's truth. Its intention is to create more cyclists, and the measure will be whether or not it hits the one million additional cyclists goal next year.

The truth of the effort is already apparent and unequivocal. And any passion about the brand among advocates whose lives have changed because of the possibilities opened up in their lives by getting on their bike is all upside.

We think Sky's innovation changes the conversation about advocacy into a challenge of delivering truth:

- **Would your brand do the campaign if nobody knew about it?** We're not recommending this as a marketing strategy, but it's an interesting question to ask yourself. The answer should be "Yes" if you want the activity founded on a secure platform.

- **Does the content have to have a thematic connection to your brand?** We think the answer can be "No," and should perhaps be so. Like Pepsi's and JPMorgan Chase's campaigns to give away grants to user-selected charities, there's truth in doing good. We think the brand benefits when it takes more responsibility for the efforts.

- **Would your advocates talk about it anyway?** Again, another "Yes" answer from us, in that the truth of an advocacy program is directly related to its utility in your consumers' experience. Your brand imprimatur, while very important, should be secondary to their desire to share.

Critics: Let's Go into Business Together

"Greenwashing" is defined as using PR or marketing to promote a misleading or untrue perception that a brand's goods or services are environmentally friendly. It has been applied liberally and oftentimes unfairly to label charitable campaigns undertaken by brands with legitimate interests in addressing environmental and community issues, but at its core it represents a rejection of the symbolism that has passed for much of brand communications over the years. Brands can't buy credibility on this issue; some purists won't even accept sustainability efforts if businesses hope to save money by implementing them (it's greenwashing if their motivations aren't exclusively altruistic). For all of the conversations enabled and opinions shared, the Internet has made it at once both easy and complicated to articulate a brand position on the environment that can hope to survive intact, or be accepted as true.

Conflicted consumers haven't helped either. Most surveys we've seen suggest that even the most environmentally conscious consumers don't like to forsake product performance benefits because they may not be wholly green and don't like paying more to substitute less effective products for them.

The recent worldwide economic malaise has made this equation even more difficult for companies challenged to truly "do something" on the environment yet do so in a financially rewarding way. The truth is hard to find on both sides of this issue.

Clorox took a distinctly different approach to this conundrum in the late 2000s when it developed its Green Works product line, and then got the Sierra Club to endorse it. "Some people might have been surprised to hear about our relationship," explained Don Knauss, Clorox CEO and chairman.

The Sierra Club must be committed to Clorox's destruction, right? The environmental group is America's oldest and has its own brand integrity based on extensive work in protecting communities and wilderness and combating global warming. The truth behind the standard conversational model would have it beat up publicly on Clorox (or any other antagonist) until some announcement or gesture toned down the debate until it flared up again.

Clorox had been working on green products in a "skunk works" research lab for years by the time Don Knauss took over in 2006. The lab team had come up with five products that were as good or better than Clorox's standard cleaning counterparts. These products used natural, renewable resources. The ingredients were both biodegradable and all but petrochemical free. No aerosol was used. Even the bleach product didn't contain bleach. You could quibble about some trace molecule here or there, but the stuff was about as environmentally responsible as you can get, particularly when you factor in the fact that the cleansers could out-clean their less Gaia-friendly alternatives.

The marketing people believed that since Clorox had sway as a multiproduct provider, major retailers would give the new products prominent shelf facings. Price would be a bit of an issue (they'd be categorized as "premium" products), but the team felt that the combination of efficacy, availability, and not-insane pricing would find a welcoming audience among consumers who were waiting for opportunities to do good without having to do much of anything different. Their only concern was that they worried consumers wouldn't believe that any of their claims were true.

Across the bridge in San Francisco, Sierra Club Executive Director Carl Pope had been working for years on his own project to shift the club's mandate from stopping bad things from happening to encouraging good things. "Instead of just saying let's boycott somebody who's making a toxic product, let's find a good product and help people who are trying to help consumers," Pope explained in a magazine story in 2008. So when Clorox came to him with its proposal, he was interested. A rigorous vetting process followed, and the Sierra Club agreed to put its logo on the packaging, promote the product line on a specially created website, and share in a percentage of the sales. It would earn more than one million dollars during the first year of the partnership.

The Sierra Club has received a lot of grief for its association with Green Works, but most of it amounts to concerns about whether the products are green *enough* to warrant the organization's involvement. One can't forget the rest of Clorox's business, which, while meeting or exceeding many environmental standards (and outperforming most products in the categories in which it competes), the simple fact is that bleach is, well, bleach.

But therein lies the truth of the Green Works partnership. It is what it is. Clorox is offering it as more than a symbolic gesture to environmental responsibility. The products are responsible and the company is transparent on how and why. For the Sierra Club's purposes, its involvement in helping sell products has helped promote environmentally responsible consumer behavior. "We have always believed that protecting and conserving the environment starts at home," Pope says on its website. "We partnered with the Green Works brand because we wanted to make affordable and effective natural cleaning products available to millions of Americans. We are thrilled that since the launch of this partnership, the natural cleaning category has more than doubled, making a real impact."

Enlisting the Sierra Club to help Clorox define the truth of its activities allowed the cleanser company to sponsor an unassailable, complete, discreet conversation among manufacturer, watchdog, and consumer. If washing with a green product is greenwashing, then it's a poster child for the practice. It's truly a good thing.

Agnostics: Substance versus Sales Engagement

Women's magazines have always traded on knowing what women want. That elusive question has been the bedrock of a huge industry of magazine sales and advertising revenue. From *Cosmopolitan*'s vision of what the young, single girl is seeking to *Good Housekeeping*'s soothing of the household matriarch, a wide offering of publications produces images and words to satisfy readers' dreams and aspirations.

This is the classic model of how the truth of a magazine brand is devised, and it's traditionally left to the instinct and genius of the editor to deliver it. A new model of journalism is evolving based on audience behavior online. The *Goodtoknow* story is one of an established women's magazine publisher transforming from a top-down editor's opinion-led publication to a bottom-up, reader-enlisted model.

IPC Media is one of the United Kingdom's publishing giants, selling millions of its special-interest glossy monthlies and mass-market weeklies. The organization had beat the odds and sustained business success through the growth spurt of the Internet in the nineties, and magazines like its music publication, *NME*, had successfully migrated online. But in the early years of the Internet, IPC had had limited online success with mass-market women's magazines. There was a huge opportunity opening up to publish online, but editors of analog magazines were guardians of their content; they rightly fought the lure of giving content away that they could still sell successfully at the newsstand.

The truth was inescapable, though. Women were beginning to look online for the inspiration, gossip, solace, and comfort that they'd previously exclusively sought in the pages of a weekly magazine. IPC sought a mass-market solution, and it turned to a young editor with an unlikely pedigree for the answer, as this project became IPC's number-one focus in 2006 and 2007.

Jolene Akehurst's background was more about news and interaction than about editorial aspirations. She graduated from a journalism course and went straight from college to a job as "the travel girl" on a local radio station. It was through joining AOL that she learned how a story could touch people and get them to connect with each other. She developed her insight of following the audience instead of telling them what they should know—believing that they, not the editors, knew best—and this came to be the core of her thinking that she calls "people's journalism." She brought this approach to IPC, where she was put in charge of a little-known site, www .goodtoknow.co.uk, which few people had ever visited.

"At the launch [of the website] there were eighteen months of readers' silence . . . the hardest thing is to feel that no one wants to talk to you," she recalled, sitting in her bright, modern office at IPC's headquarters just south of the River Thames. Her solution was to flip the model, literally, and position the website as a fellow friend of readers. Fewer editorial declarations and more of the sort of information you'd get from a friend you bump into in the supermarket parking lot, even if the substance of that interaction was brief because you're really too busy to stop and talk. Empathy for the lives of her readers mattered far more than any expert opinion about it.

While this was a profound insight, it wasn't enough to deliver truth. Her editorial team made the difference. We call what they did an "ongoing search engine optimization editorial approach." Here's how it works:

- The walls are covered with the latest from Google Analytics.
- When trending topics of interest are identified—perhaps a health issue or child care or money—Akehurst asks her writers, "How would the reader explain it to her friend in that parking lot?"
- January content reflects anxieties about weight gain, spending too much on Christmas, and gripes about the weather (gray and freezing at best).
- Valentine's Day trends earlier than the actual event because her readers enjoy the anticipation of the event, so content addresses their pragmatic optimism and then, after the holiday, shares a moan about how their significant others failed to live up to expectations.
- As a rule, the content is produced in order to win top natural search listings, not to bring to life the top-down vision of an editor.

The truth of this content is further substantiated by the tone of the magazine, which has to be affectionately lighthearted and afford readers the comfort and ability to contribute their own thoughts. This can be realized in simple touches, such as the use of language over a recent Christmas season, which skipped addressing weight gain in terms of increased obesity and health risks and instead asked if anyone else (notice the "else") was feeling that their clothes were a bit tight? The fact that debate now rages over a large number of issues on the website is testament to Akehurst's achievement.

Goodtoknow goes beyond reporting and enlists a community of readers who are also contributors and friends; they're a community that gets to shape the content, personality, and truths that make up the publication. The strategy is genuine, which is at the core of its truth. Akehurst is adamant that her readers' opinions are more important than hers, and it is reflected in every aspect of the operation. It is less strident than some online communities and less campaigning. It is a good place to find comfort and self-affirmation for a growing set of advocates enlisted in a great big digital supermarket parking lot.

Akehurst is adamant that her readers' opinions are more important than hers, and it is reflected in every aspect of the operation.

There will always be a magazine market for titles that are built on the dictates of an editorial diva, and these media will deliver that editor's own truths. Akehurst is forging a model that goes beyond that one-way consumption ("here's what I think, and tell me what you think about what I think") and instead creates a community of shared thoughts and opinions. She has found a way to enlist her readers in helping define the truth of their content.

CONFLICT RESOLUTION

One thing our age has made very apparent is that conversing itself can become the point of the conversation. Dialogue is an outcome that has inherent value, whether meaningful for brands and/or entertaining for consumers. There is also truth in this: the willingness and ability to

(continued on next page)

talk, and especially to do so openly, is considered a good thing, even if the substance of the conversation isn't particularly relevant to our own particular interests. Open is better than closed.

But it doesn't necessarily change minds, and allowing conversation (or debate) to eclipse conflict resolution makes any differences of opinion part of the truth. Just look beyond the business world to ongoing geopolitical conflicts around the world, and consider the "truth" of negotiations that go on and on without resolution. The truth behind those circumstances is that the warring positions are intractable. Now consider those that have been resolved, such as repaired marriages or, less frequently, successful corporate mergers of onetime competitors. The narrative of conflict was replaced with conciliation and agreement (however begrudging, at times), so the truth of our awareness on that topic is the truth of its resolution.

The lesson for business is that conversation is only a good thing if it leads to conclusions and actions. So your strategy should be to bring as much of that dialogue, whether positive or contentious, into your positioning. Enlisting others isn't a channel or outbound strategy but a core component of your inbound business operation. If there are conflicts to be had, have them on the front end, not after you've tried to claim the truth of your position publicly. Resolve conflicts, don't just fight them well.

Conclusion

We think there are at least two big ideas in this chapter:

First, your brand is a wiki, made up of truths from a variety of sources. Think of "content" as the generic term it is and instead consider that truths are composed of substantive experience and fact. There's no easy place where your wiki is housed because versions of it exist in each consumer and customer's mind. The mechanisms of updating it are also far more fluid than the easy keyboard entry for an online version, but we can identify and map them.

Second, the brand truth model requires that you enlist others in how you establish your truths (and not just in how you transmit them). Another word we encourage you to discard is "audience" or any permutation of it. Understanding groups of people in terms of what information matters to them and how they put it to use is a solid methodology for creating your brand wiki maps, as you could imagine them literally drawn on a whiteboard. You don't need to create new programs for their involvement, necessarily, but rather identify the activities within your business on which they will have the most to say and contribute. Your truth will be directly related to how successful you are in engaging them on the substance of those activities.

We've researched and dissected five ways to enlist others. There are more, and there may be very different ones for your particular business or industry category. Three fundamental rules apply to all of them and how you together define truth:

1. **Vested and shared outcomes.** If all you aspire to do in relating to communities is to engage their interest or entertain their fancy, your brand position will be built on a mountain of virtual sand. Truth is engagement with implications. Responsibilities. Repercussions. Your partners in defining your brand truth are more than spectators, even if they possess wonderfully supportive opinions; the strategic and creative challenge is to identify how they can share in the outcomes of your operations. The truth of their involvement will speak far more forcefully and sustainably over time. Think of those analyst reports that stand in stark contrast to others with less credibility.

2. **Make it really new.** We live in times that have rendered so many institutions discredited or outright mute, so when you enlist others you can't ask them to do the exact same things that you or your competition have done in the past. Newness—and the themes of freshness and the unsullied substance it suggests—is a core driver of truth. When Ford invited the journalists into its headquarters, the newness of that idea was itself shocking, let alone whatever information it contained. The content of truth doesn't emerge from a program or campaign but rather an idea for collaboration that might not have evidenced itself before.

3. **In-your-face honesty.** One of the things we love about the Green Works/Sierra Club partnership is that it is what it is. There are no qualifications or twisted angles, and this lets people either approve or disapprove of the effort. But the effort itself is thereby rendered wholly true. The challenge is for your brand to look beyond the easy approaches to transparency and do things that stand for themselves. Incorporating a partner into your communications is a smart way to get closer to this goal, as making even a dicey debate a part of your truth is far preferable to waiting for it to become a challenge to it. Inclusion is the name of the game these days, and in-your-face honesty can never be underused.

ENLIST OTHERS CHECKLIST

1. Which brand in your category has most third-party support? Do you know why?

2. Which one prompts the most hostility, or perhaps simply the most attention, good or bad? Do you see a correlation between levels of engagement and volume of good or bad comments?

3. How can you open up to enlist consumers in a virtual way into your marketing team?

4. Is there a new way of doing business (even if it is a niche) in partnership with others that might help your brand be seen as more truthful?

5. What are the organizations with which your brand has no relationship (or a bad one)? Why don't you have a strategy to overcome that, since they'll talk about you anyway (and plans to educate and convince them don't count)?

6. When you bring bloggers into your organization, do you have an explicit agenda or do you let them set the priorities? Are your interactions always linked to specific marketing objectives? What metrics do you possess to affirm the wisdom of these strategies?

7. If you have to identify a common ground issue for your brand and its worst detractors, what would it be? What is stopping you from developing and delivering the content to define it publicly?

8. What percentage of the coverage or buzz on your latest news announcements is truly reactive and after the fact versus achieved through your engagement strategies on the front end?

9. If you had an extra 25 percent of your employee communications budget to spend, how would you allocate it to better inform and inspire your people to deliver truth(s) about your brand? So why aren't you spending it?

10. If you surveyed your team, what organizations would they identify as being "natural" advocates or partners? If you asked them how they would create the substance of such relationships, what would they propose?

PART TWO:

CONTEXT

How you experience things is as important as the content of your experience. This was an idea forcefully touched upon by media theorist Marshall McLuhan, who published *Understanding Media: The Extensions of Man* in 1964. In it he proposed that we understand media's effect on society without the content it communicates. Content doesn't matter, according to him, insomuch that a lightbulb is a medium without any of it, yet its light still creates an environment for experience. Similarly, interacting with a television versus a newspaper are two very different things, and the qualities of such varied engagement are more important to society than the content of what folks are watching or reading.

"The medium is the message" was his famed quote, and he saw all technologies as media that extend human senses all but infinitely, connecting individuals with a global village of experiences that are at once everywhere and nowhere. His ideas still have people debating today whether he was incredibly insightful or simply a very literate charlatan (or a little bit of both).

The world has changed somewhat cataclysmically since then, and we see McLuhan's thinking in a different light. He thought very visually, and much of his writing was combined with illustrative ad imagery or custom creations of artist partners, so imagining those "extensions of man" brings to mind wires extending from someone's fingers to connect them to technology, doesn't it? Now those connections would be wireless and they would also be mobile and apparent, both explicitly and implicitly, in a variety of devices. It's doubtful that McLuhan imagined smart billboards, microblogging from a smartphone, or Wikipedia. While technology has certainly continued to disrupt as it changes how we experience it, what has become apparent since the 1960s is that content is central, both to experience and what we take away from it. Content matters, perhaps more so than he (or we) imagined, as if in a direct ratio to the diversity of media. The more we experience, the more those experiences must give us in order to be memorable and useful.

Not only does content matter (as we hope we've established in the first half of this book), but the context of experience— the where, when, and how of media—is no less important. You can't separate one from the other, as McLuhan would have argued; you can't speak truth in an untruthful way, and no seemingly truthful approach will change the fact that what you're saying is false. Our quote might be less memorable, but goes like this: "The content is the message, depending on the context."

Just imagine that picture of McLuhan's extensions, only not as outbound connectors to a global village but as inputs and influences directed at each individual consumer. There are screens and speakers and quasi-intelligent objects everywhere. On and off buttons, search query fields, and various other software tools provide a modicum of user control, but in many ways the global village is a constant, varied, and often-times inchoate presence in our lives. The context of our experiences with them is a direct determinant of what content we perceive as true. We dip into it as it dips into us.

It's not enough to speak truth anymore, if it ever was. Some media are truer than others, though it depends on where and how experienced as well as what content it contains. The second half of this book will explore some of the most successful ways brands have addressed context to deliver truth. Truthful content is the prerequisite to all of their efforts.

It's not enough to speak truth anymore, if it ever was. Some media are truer than others, though it depends on where and how experienced as well as what content it contains.

5

Be Close

One of the first qualities of context that we need to address is closeness or locality. The here-and-nowness of experience is inherent in the way we perceive things, as even our word for "sense" is based on older words for "feeling" and "understanding." Knowledge might originate anywhere in the ether but its reality—its truth—is experienced locally. Our senses are local. We're built that way. We can extend our physical sensory apparatus—writing abstract oral traditions makes them impersonal, just as technology devices let our eyes and ears experience things not within either senses' reach—but our sensory receptors are quite literally still attached to us. We have to overcome this sense of closeness, much like the people who first saw a motion picture of an approaching train and ran out screaming from the theater, thinking they were about to be run over, or why the sound of a distant thunderclap still makes us instinctively jump. Things are more real the closer they are to us.

Conversely, the more "distant" qualities are, whether calculated by space, time, or the nature of the concept, the greater chance that they'll come across as untrue. That's why describing a taste or scent is not as meaningful as experiencing them, however descriptively beautiful the imagery might be. With apologies to American politician Tip O'Neill, "all marketing is local."

Being "local" is therefore not just a quality of geophysical space. Media experiences enabled by the Internet can be very close and personal while connecting people and ideas separated by oceans of physical distance. Our research has identified five broad qualities of locality that can affect the context of truth:

- Physical
- Spiritual
- Emotional
- Intellectual
- Experiential

It's also important to remember that we're not looking at locality as a function of technology. This is different from conventional wisdom and promises of content prompts sent to smartphones keyed to geolocation, correlated with past buying habits and recognizing nearby community members and their referrals, etc. This sort of technological thinking is similar to that of Marshall McLuhan more than a half-century ago, in that technology matters more than technique. It doesn't. The only way such marvelous continuums of media experience work is if the content they contain is true, and they're configured to the way truth is understood in the context of the individual consumer's experience. We want to explore the ways that true content are matched to various contexts of nearness, of being local in expression and retention. Technology is relevant but it's not determinant. Consumers are.

Physical: The Return of Regional and Local Selling?

One of the primary effects of the twentieth century's mass media advertising revolution was to displace communications and selling that used to be conducted in person. "Local" meant in your house or at least somewhere nearby. Brushes, encyclopedias, vacuum cleaners, and insurance used to be sold door to door, and local media were used to support those efforts (if they were used at all).

Politicians still live somewhat in this world, which is why you can sometimes catch a candidate shaking hands at a subway stop, or campaign staff canvassing a neighborhood, but these activities are more the exception than the rule. Not only has the available technology helped this transformation but thinking on brands has developed along with it. The trend has been toward globalization of organizations and to homogenous advertising campaigns. Where global communications aren't in play, then they're organized upon somewhat smaller configurations, like EMEA (Europe, the Middle East, and Africa) or English-speaking countries (United Kingdom, United States, Canada, Australia).

Within the United States and the United Kingdom, national marketing and advertising campaigns are the general rule, and why wouldn't they be? The idea that you can create one central communication that fits everyone is both conceptually and financially appealing. After all, the same shops grace main streets and shopping centers. There's a Starbucks within walking distance for nearly everyone in a major town or city. It's why regional ad buys are in decline and regional-only media (like local newspapers) have been in decline for some years now in most developed nations.

So it's odd that one of the most successful campaigns in support of digital was executed door to door. Manually, so to speak.

Digital UK, the organization leading the United Kingdom's switch from analog to digital TV, was set up in 2005 to sell nothing more than an idea to approximately 34 percent of the households that still had analog TVs. It was an independent, not-for-profit organization dedicated to helping them convert to digital TV. Plus, even if you already had digital TV in the United Kingdom, you still might need to adjust your set, depending on your digital provider, and many people with digital or cable TVs for their main sets still had older analog units throughout their houses. So the challenge was far larger than simply converting the one-third of households to digital; more than 90 percent of the twenty-six million households in the United Kingdom would have to do something as a result (either buy a new set, retune, or adapt). Add to the fact that not even a charitable view of the analog audience would qualify them as "tech savvy"—it would cost most households money and the changeover wasn't a consumer-led action but rather something prompted by industry and mandated by government—and you had a big challenge combined with a big problem.

The obvious solution would be to come up with a compelling message, test it in research, and run it nationally so that everyone could be informed. A huge national campaign was a no-brainer with this kind of task. Most communications experts would tell you that a national campaign would operate most effectively and efficiently nationally, thus offering better results and value.

Beth Thoren, Digital UK's marketing director, thought differently. If the digital switchover had been on one single date for the whole United Kingdom and involved something as consistently simple as pushing a button, then she might have been tempted to consider a national campaign. But the program was rolling out region by region and transmitter by transmitter (and there were sixty-seven of those). Every household had the potential to offer different or unique circumstances, and the most likely consumers she needed to reach would be the older traditionalists who were least likely to believe what ads told them. Beyond an early warning via PR and general awareness, a national campaign had no role and risked falling on deaf or disbelieving ears.

Beth's solution was to go old school and make the case for a regional campaign supported by a hands-on road show in shopping malls and outreach through grants to local charities. Her reasoning was threefold:

First, since the technology switchover would roll out region by region, she could tag the communications to the immediacy of the effort. This would make whatever she chose to tell people far more compelling and believable than if it were in anticipation of some far-off event.

Second, despite considering the costs of regional buying, she believed she could get a better and more effective return on her marketing expenditure because the messaging could be made more locally relevant and it would enable her to "hot house" each region and thus benefit from the multiplier effect. Every penny of this public money had to be accounted for, and she was eventually able to demonstrate that her regional communications were 20 percent more effective than national.

Third, the measured rollout would give her the chance to learn as it unfolded. She could build into each region a rollout analysis using qualitative research, quantitative research, and econometric models to refine the creative mix and optimize the media plan for the next phase.

She was right. Her expectations that regional media would do better than a national buy, even at a cost per thousand premium versus national equivalents, were borne out by hitting her awareness and conversion targets in advance of each changeover, with the cost of communication per household steadily dropping. There was added power, or we'd say truth, in the message being delivered to the relevant areas at the relevant times. The Switchover Campaign road show worked right out of the chute and then got better with every stop, as the same team gathered experience as it traveled from local area to local area. Overall, the UK Digital Switchover has grown in efficiency, with the cost of communication with each household going down and thus the return on investment going up. And the critical success factor—the relentless focus on "hot housing" locally—effectively tore up the rule book for effective change through marketing. Beth and her team took a difficult and indeed largely unwelcome message and made it not only palatable but actionable. A combination of local, unmissable advertising and personal handholding made the pitch utterly true. So it was both believable and doable.

Again, the UK Digital Switchover campaign translated a digital idea into qualities that were physically local and real: regional and local ads that could key into specific actions that were supported by in-person presentations that literally walked people through the process. We say these qualities made the campaign truthful.

Spiritual: Measure My Soul

In the last chapter, we talked about the partnership between Clorox and the Sierra Club to affirm the content of the Green Works products. When it comes to environmental responsibility, there are also ways to address the context of how truth is communicated. We're particularly intrigued by the work of the Sustainable Apparel Coalition.

If you're somebody who cares about protecting the environment, you're likely interested in agriculture, whether for how it impacts protected resources and/or the ways in which it is cultivated for food and clothing. Consumer purchase decisions related to the environment must rely on the disclosures from brands, which may or may not amount to truth; as we noted, even the most genuine declarations from corporations can be discounted or disbelieved merely on their face value or due to distrust of the messenger. This is especially true when it comes to claiming a commitment to good works, or to working good, as in claims of environmental responsibility. There are independent sources of information available online, but most of them aren't qualified by much more than visits or avowals of sincerity. One consumer's sustainable behavior is another's exploitative ruse.

Much of the brand marketing response recently has been to engage in public charitable programs, focusing consumers on "meaning marketing" in which they can participate. The logic is that engaging in these shared marketing campaigns can attach the credibility and meaning to brands that the underlying businesses may not be able to establish (or perhaps don't deserve). This approach has unlocked many millions for good causes around the world, which is a fact that we applaud. But it does seem like a bit of a roundabout way of getting at the truth. If a company is going something good—whether on the environment or any other public-interest topic—shouldn't there be more direct ways of communicating such truth?

Understanding and using the objectivity of context can help in this regard, and using it to get closer to people in a spiritual way is the brilliant insight of the Sustainable Apparel Coalition.

The coalition is the brainchild of Patagonia founder Yvon Chouinard and Rick Ridgeway, the company's vice president of environmental initiatives and the coalition's original chair. Founded in 1972, Patagonia is an outdoor apparel company with a very deep and vocal commitment to environmental causes, driven by Chouinard's personal commitment to such issues. He cofounded the Conservation Alliance in 1989 to get businesses (now at 170 members) to support outdoor causes and founded 1% For The Planet in 2001, which asks companies (now at more than twelve hundred members) to commit to giving 1 percent of their revenue to environmental causes. Patagonia also runs a number of its own environmental programs, including a very transparent supply-chain process, which consumers can explore on Patagonia's website, and an outbound program called Our Common Waters.

The Sustainable Apparel Coalition has a simple but huge aspiration: to lead the industry toward a shared vision of sustainability built on an industrywide index for measuring and evaluating apparel and footwear product sustainability (as detailed in a company press release on March 1, 2011). In other words, it wants its members to prove that their brands have souls by creating a number. It is making tangible efforts real for consumers.

The indices, one each for apparel and for footwear, will include ratings from every step of the production process, from resources and cultivation to processing, manufacturing, shipping, and even displaying. Not only will consumers be able to use this tool to determine if one shirt design or shoe model is more environmentally responsible than another but designers and product makers will be able to use it to build more responsibility into their products (the same way that moviemakers edit their films with foreknowledge of ratings requirements). By signing onto this objective measure of efficacy on the issue of the environment, participating brands can translate their somewhat distant declarations of responsibility into a close-up measure that, quite literally, will be in consumers' hands, whether printed on a tag or available via a quick QR code scan on a smartphone.

We see immense truth in this endeavor and find it a great

example of taking a somewhat abstract idea—"is the brand responsible or not?"—and making a spiritual connection into something real and nearby. The truth of the index rating is rendered "local" because it externalizes a subjective experience into an objective thing that consumers can share. It doesn't matter whether you care or not about the environment, or if your brand has any relevance to the issue. Consider how this mechanism of context makes truth local:

- **Range.** It takes a spiritual quality like commitment and turns it into a measurable range of effort, literally transforming it into a good, better, best display—like hot sauces that are ranked from mild to hot but with every spicy food maker agreeing to the same assessment tool.

- **Clarity.** A two is better than a six in golf, but a higher score trumps lesser ones in all other ball-related sports. Consider how many brands declare support for causes, and even announce financial giving, without understanding how these claims fit into bigger or broader pictures. How much the company that just gave money to a good cause also spends on desserts in its executive dining room, for instance, is not as clearly obvious, and therefore the pat on the back for the company's charitable contribution might not come across as true.

- **Comparison.** The objective ranking enables apples-to-apples comparisons across product lines, which is the truth of where and how people shop. It has this quality of all the brands having agreed to live and die by the same criteria.

By delivering these qualities, the purchase decision feels local—the consumer is empowered right there and then—which connotes truth in communications. It should make you think about the various numbers you promote (speeds, sizes, whatever) in an entirely new light.

Emotional: Everyone Had a Good Time

The scene was Liverpool Station, London, at about 11 a.m.
on January 15, 2009, a day that set in statistically the most de-
pressing week of the long English winter. Out of nowhere, the
1960s hit *Shout!* starts playing over the station's loudspeakers,
and a single commuter, standing before the schedule board,
breaks into dance. Before anyone knows what's happening,
the music changes to a throbbing dance beat and a dozen
people start dancing with him. Then it morphs into a waltz
and more people join in. The music keeps jumping across
genres, each time getting new and different commuters to
dance. Mobile phones are held high to capture the moment.
Another song from the 1960s brings grandmothers to participate in the now gigantic dance. The station's main floor area
is covered with syncopated movement. Then the music hits
a crescendo and abruptly stops. The dancers walk away in all
different directions, as if a spell has been broken. Spectators
are left talking madly into their mobile phones, seemingly
unable to believe what they'd just witnessed.

To understand what had happened, you have to start a year
prior, in October of 2008. T-Mobile was feeling some pain
in the United Kingdom, despite being one of the country's
leading telecom brands. It was facing diminishing returns in
a crowded market because of a strategy that had mainly been
concerned with price cutting and offers, while its competitors
had bigger market share and higher consideration from consumers. T-Mobile was unloved.

It was then that Lysa Hardy stepped into the role of T-Mobile's
head of brand and communications. She issued an extraordinary brief to the communications team, made up of several
agencies and her own people. The challenge was to deliver a
step change in the communications by achieving three things:

- Make people think *something* about T-Mobile (many people were simply neutral or agnostic about the brand).
- Make them smile (recession was biting, winter was on the way).
- Above all else, make sure that the solution is authentic.

There is no great advertising without a great consumer insight. Lynne Ormrod led the brand development team at T-Mobile that was charged with investigating the brand's role in people's lives, and she spent days with groups of customers talking about how they used their mobile phones. What did T-Mobile's tagline, "Life's for sharing," mean to them? Ormrod began to get a feeling about people's emotional relationships with their mobile phones; they didn't just see them as tools for keeping in touch or accomplishing tasks like a laptop. The relationship was very personal, offering companionship by bringing friends and loved ones local. When in groups, people talked about how they couldn't wait to text their friends with jokes or complaints or pictures they'd just taken, like they were together, however virtually. One young woman explained how she couldn't wait to get out of the subway to send a funny picture to her best friend. As Ormrod observed the groups, she understood that there was some unique territory in everyday sharing of life's ups and downs. No other mobile brand had really gotten to grips with it.

This insight was added to Hardy's brief and then, with the creative team at Saatchi & Saatchi, they came up with the idea of staging a flashmob dance in a train station. Central to the event would be that it should be so spontaneous and real that nonactors would feel involved with it (and want to share it). The production plan was as audacious as the creative, calling for staging the dance repeat times and filming it with numerous cameras, pulling out the best, most joyous clips, and airing a three-minute advertisement special event thirty-six hours later. The speed of the turnaround was fast (from the idea sign-off in November to on-air in January), and the commitment of everyone involved was huge. Decisions were many and they had to be made quickly. We expect that this commitment is really what it takes to create truly successful advertising that enhances a customer's brand experience in an authentic manner.

The event couldn't have gone off better. The joy of the commuters surprised by the event could not have been created simply by great dancers or an accomplished director. They found it genuine and real—true—in an immediate way, just as Hardy and her team had hoped. The footage was great. The last hours before the advertisement aired were particularly tense, though, as the team predictably got right down to the wire when it came to meeting deadlines to run the spot in the center break of Channel 4's *Celebrity Big Brother*. The buzz about the flashmob event combined with paid promotion got everyone excited, if not a bit on edge. Hardy herself raced home just in time to watch the advertisement air with her family. Only then did she fully grasp what they'd accomplished.

Within seconds, texts and emails started coming in, from colleagues and acquaintances. The buzz continued to build, as did media coverage. Snippets of footage circulated across computers and smartphones. Hardy couldn't have predicted that the spot would become one of the most recognized, shared, enjoyed, and ultimately award-winning spots of 2009. Foot traffic into T-Mobile stores would double, as would the number of people searching for the brand online. Sales and market share all increased and cost per acquisition more than halved. The team would go on to create other events in the "Memorable Moments" campaign, like a giant sing-along in Trafalgar Square in April 2009, and then a musical "Welcome Back" event at Heathrow's Terminal 5 in October 2010.

Foot traffic into T-Mobile stores would double, as would the number of people searching for the brand online. Sales and market share all increased and cost per acquisition more than halved.

In each event and ensuing spot, the content obviously featured real people as well as trained dancers, and the authenticity of their involvement was priceless. They're so real that people are vying to be involved in future events. Their emotional connection with the campaign is very real.

Many advertisers and creative agencies work on briefs that are intended to deliver such a connection between the brand and the target audience. Take any major sporting event on television and most ads that run during the breaks are either trying for humor or epic emotions, or both. It's our view that few of them truly manage it despite big production qualities and big production budgets.

Why is the emotional context of the T-Mobile campaign so true?

- **It didn't try to own the content.** The truth is inherent in the experiential moment, not in an abstraction somehow linked to the brand. Arguably, making such a connection might not have come across as legitimate from a brand that had no prior association. T-Mobile didn't take an easy solution, however; it's not easy to combine authenticity with commercial delivery, and setting out to cheer up a nation in the doldrums of winter is no small task. But the effort was sincere on its own, and therefore it was true.

- **The experience spoke for itself.** The very shooting and editing style spoke truth in a way that no copy or tagline could. When we watch the spots, we feel as though we're there, perhaps contemplating what we would do had someone broke out into song or dance standing next to us. For all of the tightly scripted narratives intended to evoke emotions from viewers, this experience seemed almost unadulterated. It didn't tell us it was true—it showed us. We felt the emotion.

- **It was authentic so it had legs.** User "HecticGlenn" posted this comment on YouTube where extra footage of the dance and the other events can be viewed: "Just got back from coming home from uni, through Liverpool Street Station. I got wondering why 5 or so people were dancing. I went to look, then *everyone* started dancing. I had to run for cover to avoid the waltz. Amazing display, really caught me by surprise." Experiences of the event almost constituted news footage.

Intellectual: Robots Playing Soccer

In terms of the do-it-yourself (DIY) movement, "Roomba soccer is a good illustration of what's possible," said Dale Dougherty, founder and publisher of *Make* magazine. Roomba is a little self-propelled robot home vacuum cleaner. A community of users hacked into them and reprogrammed the devices to play soccer. Their games got on Roomba's corporate radar, and the company embraced the idea by providing the interface so those hackers didn't have to break in. Then they started selling kits so users could build other applications. Roombas have been linked to everything from Google (creating a "Gagglebot" that shoots web video as it vacuums) to Microsoft Kinect motion controllers, so users can point to spots that need attention.

Dougherty is one of the founders of O'Reilly Media, a publisher and events company focused on the high-tech space and responsible for the first website to feature ads, in 1993. He founded *Make* in 2005.

"So much of what's been going on over the past decade or so has been about personal empowerment," he continued. "Technology is helping people learn to take more control and have more responsibility over their lives. It can be as simple as possessing the tools to, say, book your own air travel. It changes how you approach such tasks, and it also challenges you to rely on other people. You don't just do things but start to develop enthusiasm for doing them."

Dougherty also saw people taking control of their technology, taking the ideas of customization and personalization that are central to computers and applying them to other areas of their lives, like cars or home appliances. Community was apparently hard-wired into such endeavors, almost as if people instinctively used the computer concept of "open source" to help one another to build things: homemade rockets, old TVs adapted to display light shows, you name it (and that's the point). Dougherty realized that the enthusiasm and sense of play of such "makers" of things wasn't just a fad but perhaps a new standard for defining the relationship between consumer and what he or she consumes. *Make* magazine and its annual Maker Faire festivals were created to give these enthusiasts a place to learn and share ideas.

"There's something very close, very personal about making something," he told us. "The involvement and enthusiasm are authentic in a way that simply buying and using something can't touch."

By definition, building or modifying a device or object is also *local*; to be "hands on" you have to be able to touch it with your hands, and we think also that this idea of literally creating something is an expression of truth. To hack something you have to know how it works, which goes far beyond simply absorbing the user information provided by marketers. The same goes for building something from scratch. Modifying, re-purposing, enhancing, and extending the utility of the things we use in our daily lives redefines them in terms of actuality. For every enthusiast who hacks GameBoy to play music, a thousand people customize their Internet browsers or the criteria for syncing their smartphones with their computers. Their accomplishments are the stuff of real community, sharing the truth of what they've done so others can do it, too.

Dougherty continued:

> Most technology products still come with a warning that if you open it up, you void the warranty. This is the exact opposite of empowerment, and it limits use to whatever purposes the marketers dreamt up. There's no way to anticipate how objects will be used and shared in the real world until they're being used and shared in the real world. Like mobile phones in cars; that interface took years for car companies to figure out, and some still don't get it. Maybe that's on purpose? Roomba saw the opportunity to acknowledge their users' involvement, and use it as a mechanism to supporting community. I wonder why more marketers don't think that way.

So do we. We marketers spend so much time trying to come up with ways to make our messages believable through creativity, when the reality of ownership and usage is both local and unquestionably true. A shower gel buyer washes with the product in her daily shower. A beer drinker has his favorite glass and serving temperature. A family vacation is constructed of many customized activities. Every brand promise gets translated into immediately tangible and unique outcomes, and often these results aren't the ones we necessarily promised. While not making permanent changes to the products and services they're using (though controlling their own use), *aren't all consumers makers?*

The idea that consumers can do a better job of defining the utility for a product or service is intellectually honest and therefore inherently true.

The DIY phenomenon has significant implications for marketers of any consumer product. Why couldn't a laundry detergent encourage users to share ways they enhance or focus stain-removing qualities? Couldn't an insurer more aggressively get a community of policyholders to use better insulation or fire-retarding materials for interior fixtures? What about a food product going beyond an ingredients list to sharing how they interact, and thereby perhaps getting consumer feedback on new tastes or effects? Shouldn't online communities of users be encouraged to talk to one another about applications of their products, not simply their opinions about them?

Shouldn't online communities of users be encouraged to talk to one another about applications of their products, not simply their opinions about them?

There's a caveat here, of course, and that's the risk of asking people to do things that they're simply not qualified to do. Recent experiments in asking consumers to select soda pop or cheese cracker flavors have only served to prove that there's often a difference between what people say they want and what they'll ultimately do. But the reality of getting people involved in customizing the products they've bought—making them truly a part of their local environments—is a powerful idea worthy of a lot more testing.

"So much of what's on TV seems so fake, and that most definitely includes supposed reality TV programs," Dougherty said. "When it works, it works because it gets people involved with their minds and their hearts. So all media experience is DIY, up to a point. If we can get their hands involved in making things, that experience gets more real."

Experiential: Do as God Commands

Speaking of laundry detergent, Procter & Gamble provides a great example of how envisioning the way consumers experience a product, from awareness to sampling and purchase, can affect how truthfully it comes across.

Back in 2005, P&G in Israel had recently acquired Biomat Detergent from Unilever. Biomat was considered a price-based brand and had significant market share among the often economically challenged Haredi Jews (an ultra-Orthodox community whose male members are prohibited by their religious faith from working). The company wanted to relaunch the brand but it faced some significant institutional obstacles: most notably, Haredim own no televisions or radios and are all but uninterested in mainstream print media. They also give no credence to traditional advertising messages; there is nothing a secular marketer could tell them that is true beyond the actuality of retail price.

P&G's solution was quite novel. The Haredi are a tightly knit community that follow strict rules of dress and conduct. One of those rules is a requirement to help the needy, whether through donations or good works. So P&G hit on the idea of enabling the donation of used clothing washed with Biomat. The company would make no promise beyond the declaration that it would clean clothes and then distribute them to those in need. To prove its point, it would equip a truck with a washing machine and send it into Haredim neighborhoods to do the cleaning right there and then. Street postings and in-store signage notified residents of the opportunity to make donations, and inserts in Orthodox newspapers supported it (they weren't ads, per se, but rather notices in the old tradition of advertisements).

When the truck arrived at a designated stop, Haredim were waiting with sacks of clothing. Many of them stayed to watch the washing process, especially if it was a nice day to be outside. The truck was appropriately and obviously branded with Biomat, of course. Subsequently, Biomat's share of sales with these consumers increased by nearly 50 percent. The campaign was an unmitigated success. It won Procter & Gamble top honors at the 2005 Cannes Lions International Advertising Festival, and has been referenced as one of many examples of effective "cause marketing." We think this label misses the real impact of the strategy.

It wasn't a cause marketing campaign. It was a truth campaign. The experience was true, and here's why:

- **It was thematically "attached" to consumers, not the brand.** A foundational premise of cause marketing is that brands should pick philanthropic activities that would matter to their target audiences (thematically meaningful to them, while keeping true to the brand) and then invite or enable consumers to contribute to those causes. Doing so attaches meaning to brands. Biomat did nothing of the sort, however, instead opting to embrace an activity already undertaken by the Haredi community. Its position wasn't "we support giving clothes to the needy," but rather "we support your efforts." The concept wasn't about a cause or about a brand. It was about consumers and what they already were doing.

- **Its action had meaning.** Doing something is inherently more genuine and meaningful than thinking about or otherwise enabling someone else to do something. Volunteers get a dose of truth directly from their ministrations. Arguably, Biomat offered to do something that was getting done anyway (washing clothes prior to donation) and asking to be a part of that activity let the brand participate in the meaning derived from that activity. It didn't attempt to change or redirect the meaning of the activity. The campaign wasn't focused on an external benefit or claiming association with a cause.

- **There were no brand promises.** By not trying to attach overtly the good works to its brand, Biomat made no follow-on promise to the Haredim. We hope there were discount coupons involved, though, because the ultimate takeaway from the campaign should have been that Biomat does a great job of cleaning clothes. If it accomplished this when washing the clothes destined for donation, then this truth was unassailable. It works. No connection to higher goods or causes was required to prompt purchase (as the sales results evidence). The experience was true because nothing that could be proven false was promised.

AN ORGANIC METAPHOR

Have you bought fresh produce (or locally created art) from a neighborhood stand recently? It's quite the trend, both in the United States and the United Kingdom, for local producers and artisans to set up booths on a regular day of the week on a seasonal basis—every Saturday morning during the summer, for example—and sell their wares to the local community. These farmers' markets, art shows, and similar activities draw on so many qualities of being "local," from economics to philosophy (and friendship).

(continued on next page)

What if a context for the truth of your brand is like setting up a local produce stand? We know it's a reach, but think about the implications:

- **Physical.** You can't call this one in, and nobody wants to watch your produce glisten on an HD flatscreen. Your brand needs to be present in the consumers' locality.
- **Spiritual.** What is it about your stand that connects with the beliefs of your customers? You need to know what matters to them and then address it versus trying to borrow it from some external source or agency.
- **Emotional.** Wanting to connect with your brand is what turns need into action. Does your stand do something right there and right then for your customers?
- **Intellectual.** It has to make sense that you're there, so selling industrial widgets probably doesn't work for your stand. What does?
- **Experiential.** The local fair usually has a beginning and an end, giving people a reason to experience it. How is your brand establishing its incentives to act?

Conclusion

Are you thinking differently about what the idea of "local" means? When it comes to perceiving truth, it has little if anything to do with technology and much more with the context of why it's presented. Does it make an emotional link or an intellectual one? Is it an idea or a passion? The contexts of how truths are made local depend on the answers to such questions, and you should have seen some common themes emerging from our case histories of how truth can be made "local," such as:

- **The less said the better.** "If you have to try too hard to convince me of something, it probably isn't true," or so the old adage goes. Something is all but self-evidently local, like the T-Mobile flashmob in Liverpool Station. Brands should spend less time trying to apply meaning to context and more time enabling the context itself to have meaning. Truth is experienced far more often than it's argued.

Brands should spend less time trying to apply meaning to context and more time enabling the context itself to have meaning. Truth is experienced far more often than it's argued.

- **Do things.** "Hands on" speaks certain truth when all other avenues for experience are questionable. For something to be local it has to be tangible, at best in a tactile, physical sense, and at least in a way that allows people to feel the presence of ideas, concepts, or activities near them. Biomat didn't talk about the truth of its commitment to its consumers' charitable works. It drove the truck right up to their doors and did it.

- **Use multiple senses.** The more senses someone can use to perceive, the more likely what they experience will seem true; put differently, truth is multidimensional, and things that are nearby can be experienced in sight, sound, touch, etc. This can mean using different experiential channels, like the way the UK Digital Switchover campaign relied on a combination of print, online, and in-person promotion. All of the channels were united in providing different perspectives on the same actionable truth. Everything was local.

- **Use multiple emotions.** So much of online engagement relies on humor, and a joke with no context or follow-on can come across as quite true (i.e., if expectations are for no truth, you can't be disappointed). As we've shown in this chapter, there are many emotions that can be used to communicate truth, including no emotion whatsoever, as in the case of the DIY phenomenon (though enthusiasts are certainly emotional, the nature of the context of their involvement is very matter-of-fact).

- **Give immediate feedback.** Waiting represents distance across time, so many of the cause marketing campaigns that rely on reaching a goal offer delayed gratification, which, to us, seems like a risk of being unfulfilled or seeming untrue. Local means "here and now," and most of the examples we found of activities that communicate truth did so by providing immediate feedback (or nearly so): the clothes washed, apparel tag read and understood, electronic gizmo disassembled.

- **Be sharable.** Truth makes for horrible secrets, whether as "burdens of truth" that should be known or the "ugly truths" from which people must be protected. T-Mobile was a genius to realize that a quality of local truth is that it's something that people would want to share; therefore, the company crafted an experience that provided that quality. Nobody shoots something with his or her smartphone to declare it didn't happen.

- **Make no promises.** Perhaps one of the most challenging realizations we had in researching the nature of locality and truth was in how much it contradicted the idea of a brand promise. The certainty of "here and now" almost obviates the need to make promises for "and then over there." Brands that were successful using the context of locality to communicate truth did so without adding additional content about what would come next; in fact, such promises would have denigrated the truth of the efforts. Local truth speaks for itself, which is one of the reasons why it can be so powerful.

BEING CLOSE CHECKLIST

1. Do you tailor your communications to make them locally relevant?

2. Which brand in your competitive set is closest emotionally to the consumer? How is that accomplished, and how much of it is proprietary (versus just smart marketing)?

3. How could a promotion deliver a benefit beyond pricing that means something to the consumer?

4. Have you considered communicating with micro-local copy?

5. Could you make heroes of your employees in their own communities?

6. Is your product recyclable, meaning is it useful in a secondary or tertiary market? How involved are you in those activities?

7. Does your brand marketing give consumers truths upon which they can take immediate personal action? Think back to the Biomat example and consider how you could deliver promotions that didn't just entertain but meant something to your consumers.

8. How much of your marketing content is sharable because it's personally useful versus funny?

9. How much of your marketing content addresses the immediate lives of your consumers versus delivering points about your product or service?

10. If your consumers didn't have your product closely meshed into their lives, what would they be going without?

6

Find a Truth Turning Point

It was a chilly UK October morning in 2010 when the nation awoke to shocking news: Wayne Rooney, the nation's most gifted soccer player, wanted to leave Manchester United FC, the nation's most successful club. Rooney hadn't had the best of years in 2010, and neither, therefore, had his fans. Expected to be the man who led England to World Cup glory that summer in South Africa, he'd played indifferently and had a colder reception from fans than other players, partly because expectations were so high and his performance was so low. Added to this were the typical speculative stories in the tabloid papers about his private life, and reports of an injury that stopped him from being on the team and threw Manchester United into turmoil. "Sources" revealed that Rooney had absolutely made the irrevocable decision to

move and that his departure might take him all of across town to United's immediate rivals, Manchester City. After the story broke, fans congregated at Rooney's home, wearing hoodies and balaclavas to warn him off, with reports of one placard threatening, "Join City and you're dead!"

It was a typical story of celebrity, skill, and lots of money, and just the sort that plays out in the popular media in most developed countries. The names and sports might differ but the narrative is the same—part Greek tragedy and part sleazy soap opera—and it always comes down to incomprehensibly large sums of cash. Its plot is somewhat timeworn and certainly predictable, so the next episode of the story was fairly obvious. Manchester United would issue some inert, emotionless statement devoid of any real information, and instead throw its weight into behind-the-scenes maneuvering that would appear as leaked drips and purposefully revealed drabs until the story reached its end.

Only it didn't happen that way. But before we get to what happened, you need to know something about the other lead character in this tale.

Manchester United's manager, Alex Ferguson, had long been a controversial figure in England's soccer scene (called football in the United Kingdom), a hero to some (but not to all) and otherwise impossible to ignore. One of the things he was (and is) notorious for was his view that no player is bigger than the club. Ferguson had once remarked, "If footballers think they are above the manager's control, there is only one word to say: good-bye." Commentators suggested that it was this attitude that led to the departure of several soccer heroes, including David Beckham and Ruud van Nistelrooy. Complicating the plot was that while he was saying good-bye to some players still at the peak of their game, Ferguson was leading United to enormous success in tournaments.

You can just imagine the conflict most UK soccer fans expected to witness. Ferguson's inflexible, one-for-all approach

had finally met its match in a spirited but uneven player, and
Rooney would portray himself as the victim of bad management. Rooney's reputation approached what *The Guardian*'s
website called "talismanic" status for fans, for many of whom
soccer is of paramount importance. (A famous quote from
Liverpool FC's legendary manager Bill Shankly in the 1960s
encapsulated this passion when he said, "Someone said to me,
'To you football is a matter of life or death!' and I said, 'Listen,
it's more important than that.'")

For his part, Ferguson was famous for being tightlipped
around journalists, having refused to give any interviews to the
BBC (unlike every other soccer manager) ever since the network ran a documentary on his closely guarded personal life.

So it was absolutely unexpected when Ferguson opened up
to the camera and, in an interview with MUTV (the club's
own channel), admitted after days of speculation that the
story about Rooney wanting to leave was true. The language
Ferguson used and the tone of voice left no doubt that he was
speaking from the heart. This wasn't a negotiation, there were
no Machiavellian mind games going on. "I was dumbfounded,"
he said about the moment he'd read about Rooney's plans. "I
couldn't understand it at all because only months before he'd
said he was at the biggest club in the world and he wanted to
stay for life. I was shocked."

It was real and therefore it was true. The speech that followed was a turning point. Ferguson went on: "I had a meeting
with the boy and he reiterated what his agent had said. He
wanted to go. I said to him, 'Just remember one thing: respect
this club.' I don't want any nonsense from you, respect your
club."

Ferguson explained that he was disappointed in the media
response after all the care and nurture that the club had given
Rooney, including financial advice. He said that this was a key
part of Manchester United's tradition of trust and loyalty between managers and players, going right back to the days of

Sir Matt Busby (the club's legendary manager in the 1950s and '60s).

Ferguson continued: "There's been no falling out. That's why we need to clarify the situation now for our fans. . . . There's no [specific] offer on the table for Wayne [at the moment] because they're not prepared to listen to an offer. But there's always an offer there for Manchester United to negotiate with a player. That's still there."

Ferguson's statement came out on a Tuesday. Three days later, Rooney signed a new five-year contract with Manchester United with a big salary increase (he doubled it to 180,000 pounds a week), and he made a public and apparently sincere commitment to prove his value for the money to his team and his fans.

It remains to be seen whether Ferguson's decision was the right one for the team (United's performance has been spotty as of the writing of this book), and we'll likely never know what went on behind the scenes. Was the manager's speech scripted? It sure didn't sound that way; rather, it overturned shunning the truth and speaking vaguely that has become the convention in professional sports. Most players and managers speak in code. So, for instance, when the player says that he needs a club to "match his ambitions" we all know he means he wants more money, or if he wants to "win a championship," he'll likely sacrifice that dream for, yup, more money.

We think the story is illustrative of at least two things:

- Sometimes letting a story play as expected isn't the best way to tell it.
- Individual, specific moments can sometimes speak truth far better than lengthy arguments or narratives.

The power of such moments challenges many of our preconceptions about the nature of marketing and branding, and of social media in particular. As communicators, we like to tell stories, perhaps since we're trained in liberal arts. We gravitate to imagery that should or must be deconstructed, narratives that have plots to follow, and jokes with punch lines that aren't always obvious. We see our efforts as making cases by weaving ongoing, somewhat linear conversations in which consumers will not only participate but also help build, follow, and ultimately connect the dots to the conclusions we've envisioned. As we've explored earlier in this book, the process of truth-telling is a viable and important strategy. It's one way of getting to the truth, even if it doesn't mean that having a "conversation" is an absolute good, or that it is synonymous with truth.

It's also not the only way to get there. Our research across multiple channels suggests that it is the "moments," not necessarily the conversation, that get consumers to truth more quickly and easily. We've dubbed them "Truth Turning Points," or "TTPs." If the process of truth-telling is an important way to look at your content, TTPs are a strategic way to understand how you encapsulate and present it.

What are TTPs?

- They're moments (or a series of moments) that are self-evident and understandable.
- They literally command attention and speak unadulterated, obvious truth. We're not advocating quips or shorthand but rather ways in which our interaction with consumers enables them to immediately perceive authenticity and what's true.
- Such moments can be efficiently delivered via digital tools but the truth they communicate has everything to do with the specific substance of those interactions, not any broader belief in the magic or purposes of technology or storytelling. Your creative execution might weave a great narrative, but it's often one or more TTPs that do all the heavy lifting.

In this case, the parts can be greater than the sum.

One way of understanding TTPs is to consider how effective and popular *behavioral targeting* has become. Behavioral targeting is a digital marketing tactic that uses the veracity of specific actions to identify consumer intentions. It's the reverse of what we're talking about, but the logic is illustrative: if a consumer is visiting XYZ site or clicking on some link or ad, his or her intentions can be extrapolated from that and messages targeted at them subsequently are more likely to work. Now imagine *flipping* that idea and purposefully creating those moments with behaviors that cause unique connections, observations, or awareness. Let's call it *behavior prompting.*

There are specific ways in which TTPs work, and they all center on challenging expectations with your business behavior and/or that of your target audience(s). Ferguson's breakthrough moment was one way to create a TTP. In this chapter we'll explore other instances of truthful moments without getting entangled with terms like "engagement," "user-generated content," "conversation," or any of the other labels that we believe sometimes obscure what's really going on. It's not about the conversation, exclusively, but also about the moments your brand creates irrespective of medium.

We've identified through our research six broad ways to create TTPs, though the list is by no means exclusive:

1. Ignore the script
2. Break the format
3. Exceed the platform
4. Expand the brief
5. Be the quote
6. Interrupt a journey

Let's look at cases that explore and support each of these strategies.

Commercials That Aren't, and Movies That Are

It's November 2010 and when the film starts, we see that a movie theater audience is politely enduring a somewhat cheesy advertisement for microwave popcorn. Then, suddenly, when one of the characters in the spot (a small child) starts to choke, the actors playing the parents seem at once terrified and paralyzed. Some of the people in the audience shift uncomfortably in their seats as the crisis doesn't resolve itself. The mother is insane with terror now, turning to the camera and begging for help. A young woman in the theater audience stands up and says she'll pitch in, runs behind the screen, and then reappears inside the commercial. She takes the choking kid in her arms and thumps her on the back, dislodging the popcorn to the relief of everyone around her. The screen displays an advertisement encouraging everyone to be better prepared for emergency health situations, brought to you by the United Kingdom's St. Johns Ambulance. As the room goes dark, the young woman reappears and returns to her seat to the sound of impromptu applause.

American consumer electronics retailer Best Buy did something similar late last decade when it also sponsored public service announcements before movies; the spots looked like actual movie trailers until the characters were interrupted by a ringing mobile phone, which moved them to address the audience and ask them to turn off their phones before the show started.

These are just two examples of TTPs that break the format of a medium in order to communicate truth, whether it's that of the personal responsibility for saving lives or not bothering fellow moviegoers. The shared connection to cinema is purely coincidental; you've seen TTPs in a variety of media experiences:

- Characters in the TV comedy hit *The Office* address the camera as if they're not actors but subjects of a documentary. This makes them seem more real and their actions more truthful, doesn't it?

• Punk rock bands established their truths by violating the formatted structure of live concert performances—performers on the stage in front of an audience—and flinging themselves into the crowds or, in the case of bands from The Who to The Clash, smashing their instruments after playing them.

Welsh fiction writer Jasper Fforde turned the format of the fiction novel upside down with his *Thursday Next* series, in which characters use footnotes to communicate outside the stories, which means using actual footnotes to the text in a gloriously new way.

Actually, advertising has been somewhat self-aware ever since early radio and TV actors delivered sponsorship and commercial messages while in character. American TV series *Marcus Welby, M.D.* actor Robert Young famously starred in a 1970s commercial that began with him admitting, "I'm not a doctor, but I play one on TV. . . ."

Note that acknowledgment or awareness of a format doesn't necessarily break through it and deliver a TTP, however entertaining the moment might be. The St. Johns and Best Buy cases illustrate the three primary qualities of format breaking that help to yield truth: the interruption is organic, characters remain in character, and the narrative is consistent. Let's look briefly at each of these.

1. **The interruption has to be organic and emerge from within the format**, not violate or disturb it from outside. Interruptions are simple enough, but usually look contrived. The St. Johns Ambulance spot broke the movie/commercial format, but it was as if it grew out of it to deliver on the truth of its message, which was, "There's no such thing as spectators in a health emergency."

2. **The characters must remain in character**, not reveal themselves to be something else (which then calls into question what they claimed to be in the first place, whether overtly or implicitly). When the TV actor admits that he only plays a doctor on TV, his truthful declaration only reminds us that he's otherwise a faux doctor. Contrast that with the actors in the Best Buy trailer who stay within character to tell us something particularly true ("Turn off your mobile phone!").

3. **The narrative needs to be consistent and finished**, not broken and then left undone or chaotic. The change needs to occur without it making viewers (or listeners) overly conscious of change. It's easy to blow up any format, and the mere act of blowing it up tells us nothing. By getting the same format to tell us something different, however, change can be a tool for telling truth.

Exceed the Platform: Eat Mor Chikin

Another avenue to TTPs involves not so much breaking a format as it does **exceeding a platform**, and by that we mean doing more—conceptually and creatively—than would have been expected, and in the process, inventing a moment that speaks truth.

Chick-fil-A is an American fast-food restaurant chain specializing in chicken, having all but invented the niche as a counterpoint to the popular hamburger-dominated chains with which it grew up (McDonald's was a contemporary, while Burger King came a few years after Chick-fil-A was founded). The category was (and is) a highly competitive one, as price points are fairly low while menu offerings are somewhat similar; regardless of what the sandwiches, fries, or cups of soda are called, the configurations are identical. This is one of the main reasons why marketing for these brands has relied so heavily on creative invention and the size of the media buy, giving Americans memorable jingles, mascots, and toys with purchase. It is consistently one of the costliest categories in which businesses compete and regularly accounts for one of the top five largest ad expenditures (2010 was more than six billion dollars). Within this marketplace Chick-fil-A has returned forty-three consecutive years of sales growth, with 2010 sales up 11 percent and same-store sales up more than 5.5 percent over the year prior.

It's a private company, so it doesn't report or break out its expenses, but we estimate that Chick-fil-A's marketing expenditure is a fraction of what its competitors spend. In this age of digital communication, it still spends a large percentage of its budget on outdoor billboards, and it works. The company has other issues with its marketing, but it sure knows how to create a TTP.

We give you "Eat Mor Chikin" or, rather, Chick-fil-A has given us this phrase and made it the linchpin of its branding and marketing strategy since 1995. The idea was simple: cows want consumers to eat more chicken. The first billboard featured a black-and-white cow sitting atop another one, holding a paintbrush and imperfectly scrawling the words "eat more chikin" on the otherwise blank expanse of the billboard. It has since been applied to a variety of media, such as in-store and radio, but outdoor still seems to form the backbone of the campaign. While its competitors have repeatedly swapped slogans and creative concepts, experimented with social media campaigns, and turned to various celebrities or sports sponsorships to get at their brand differences, Chick-fil-A has stayed amazingly constant on its commitment to "Eat Mor Chikin" (it dabbles in sponsorships and online, but not at near the level of its competitors).

Why does it work? The standard marketing analysis is that it's a great integrated marketing idea. It has won advertising awards, and its cows were immortalized in 2007 on New York's Madison Avenue Advertising Walk of Fame. "Chick-fil-A came to The Richards Group with big dreams and a small budget," said Stan Richards, founder and principal for The Richards Group, according to Chick-fil-A's press materials. "They needed a campaign that would help them raise awareness and compete against the big burger chains, while preserving their unique philosophies and culture."

We think the campaign goes far beyond great marketing and works because the obviously false, impossible, and benefit-empty idea of cows lobbying for a diet choice is *true*. The company's billboards are TTPs because they go beyond the typical limitations of a marketing platform to prompt truth. Here's how:

- **Tangible idea.** The Chick-fil-A concept requires no deconstruction, no interpretation, and no association or nuance. It's an idea and slogan based on an action verb— do something—which means it prompts no debate about the message or challenges to its veracity. While an expert could tell you that the cows portrayed are dairy cows, not the type used for meat, the truth of cows, generally, having an issue is obvious. It's an idea you can choose to consider but not something you need to believe or not.

- **Obviously commercial.** The company wants all of us to give it money in exchange for its chicken sandwiches, and it spends money to put this pitch in front of us. Again, a TTP emerges because of this transparency; consumers don't have to agree or disagree with the reasoning or punch line, but can simply say "yes" or "no." There's truth in such simplicity.

- **Reasonable fantasy.** Okay, cows can't think or talk, and they certainly couldn't paint billboards, yet the idea behind the campaign seems utterly true because cows destined to become hamburger meat *would* say "eat mor chikin" if they could. The company reaches beyond the normal approach to content for a billboard slogan and finds real truth in a consciously artificial way.

- **Medium appropriate.** Chick-fil-A resists the natural (and common) tendency to work around the limitations of a medium and instead crafts a pitch that doesn't make consumers focus on the billboard-*ness* of it all. (Some of the billboards are 3D and feature cows climbing around them, but it's not central to the creative concept.)

You'll hear us argue throughout this book that we believe social technologies have reminded us that all media are tools for conversation, and the "Eat Mor Chikin" billboards provide TTPs that contribute to such an ongoing dialogue. They do it by extending the limitations of a media platform (really, we're well into the twenty-first century . . . billboards?) and in doing so find a way to communicate a message that is completely true.

Video Didn't Kill the Radio Star

One director of marketing at a big TV network recently described her job as promoting "a brand that delivers experiences," which is an elegant way of saying **expand the brief**. It's an interesting insight into another of the ways TTPs are within reach of any brand, as well as what they mean for a media owner delivering programming.

"Consumer engagement" is a term that fills us with a great deal of concern because it is enormously imprecise. It smacks of the great persuasive job that ad agencies did in the bad old days when they would try and convince a client that awareness was the only advertising metric to worry about. No sales? *No problem*, they'd say, since the point was that your audience saw your ad, which meant that at some point they'd buy your product.

Not true. We've known for decades that without a more tangible short-term effect there will be no long-term anything worth measuring, yet today's pundits often talk about consumer engagement with the same vague hopes. We know that it is consumers buying stuff that matters (it's almost embarrassing to have to say it, as if there were a cogent argument against it). If you can deliver great brand moments—TTPs—to consumers, then they are very certain to shell out money on that brand, short- and long-term.

We've found great examples of experimentation on this front among media owners, not just consumer brands, especially as they endeavor to sell TTPs/experiences to advertisers rather than just eyeballs and exposure. The organization that has changed its approach most recently and most fundamentally in this direction is London's Capital Radio, which is one of the city's top pop music radio stations. It has been around for decades and most Londoners in marketing and media (that is marketing and media people who grew up within Greater London) grew up listening to the channel at some point in their teens. They, as we all do, eventually grew up and away from the station and its programming, but the channel has done a very successful job of reinventing itself and making itself relevant for generation after generation of London teenagers.

In 2008, the station was bought by a new consortium, Global Radio, and the new management team brought a new sales approach: the brand was a music and entertainment business, not just a radio station. To realize this new perspective, Stephen Miron, the group CEO, brought in a team with experience from other media and rekindled the creativity of the existing radio sales team.

Miron, speaking from his sunny offices in London's Leicester Square, talked about the need not just to improve his team's selling techniques but the overriding need to get a step change in culture and self-belief. Radio has always had trouble increasing its share of the media revenue cake in the United Kingdom and, as the band The Buggles declared on MTV's inaugural music video in 1981, "Video Killed the Radio Star." Only it hadn't. What struck Miron and his team, including Mike Gordon, managing director, commercial, was how much more flexible the content was in commercial radio than in newspapers where both had spent a significant part of their early careers, and how little they were doing beyond teeing up songs for listeners.

In the station's defense, its simple proposition—the greatest, freshest tunes from the world's biggest artists—had delivered results through reaching a very defined audience in a very specific way. Global took this position as a starting point for creating events (what we term TTPs) that brought audiences together in new ways beyond reaching them only as radio listeners. Through this mission, the Capital Balls were born.

The Summertime Ball and the Jingle Bell Ball, with their party atmospheres, were fabulous get-togethers for teenage London. And the balls made sense from a commercial perspective. They were a chance for artists to perform their hits live, they brought in revenue from ticket sales, and they were a great opportunity for the record labels due to sampling: someone might buy a ticket because he or she was a huge Rihanna fan but wind up loving, say, Chipmunk after seeing his act for the first time. It also was an opportunity to promote the station by offering weeks and weeks of chances for listeners to win VIP tickets or the chance to meet your pop idol—experiences that money can't buy, and lastly, it brought about multiple sponsorship opportunities for advertisers, who also could attend the balls and see the audience interact with their brands in the flesh. Watching an arena full of teenagers playing along with the famous Cadbury eyebrow advertisement in order to win a Guinness World Record for mass participation could only serve to impress the marketing team with the power of the medium.

Gordon's sales proposition became the ability to make a real difference to a brand by activating excitable teens with these TTPs. Over a two-year period, when one of radio's traditionally biggest clients, the UK government, pretty much stopped spending during the recent recession, Global's profits weren't hurt. In fact, they nearly doubled due to Gordon's marketing initiatives.

Another example of expanding the brief via TTPs comes from the award-winning Xbox "Lips" campaign. Lips was the latest karaoke game from Xbox in 2009. Christmas is an awfully cluttered market for games, although television is clearly a great medium for showing the fun of a karaoke game. So some TV spots would have been an okay answer for this marketing challenge. But worries around cutting through and getting to that much desired number-one spot in the gaming chart meant that the standard marketing solution wasn't satisfactory and Global Radio won the opportunity to pitch for the campaign.

The team at Global, led by sales director Ed Chalmers, put together an expanded solution that included a six-week road show across the United Kingdom with thousands of people playing the game across the country, and a television advertisement specially edited from all of the footage recorded from the road show, and then broadcast with just one spot on mainstream television. The biggest TTP of the concept was that the road shows would create huge karaoke parties that would give teenage girls the opportunity to star in their own music video, which would appear in the special commercial placed halfway through *The X Factor* on ITV (the biggest show at the time, on the biggest UK channel).

Tim Ferris, a ten-year Global Radio veteran, had a passion for breaking out of the normal constraints of how the station viewed its role vis a vis experience. He knew that a classic planner would have kicked this idea out before it was even pitched, but he and his team sold the idea hard to Xbox and its media agency, and ended up with one of the biggest projects of his career at that time.

Ferris organized a road show to travel up and down the United Kingdom and shoot video footage of people singing along to the game. This was turned into a giant mash-up of the song that was broadcast at Global's Jingle Bell Ball and in the center break of *The X Factor*. In addition, the *Lips* website let people download their own individual performances and mash them up however they liked, whether with other backup singers and/or with a famous singer. Group CEO Miron can't hide his pride in the work his team did in pushing the ideas and taking them almost "ridiculously far."

Fun and interactive, this huge-scale project delivered. There was space sold, certainly. There were audience ratings on radio as part of the package sold, indeed. But more than anything, Global went beyond the brief of a radio station and went from selling "listening" to selling "audience experiences." These moments were TTPs that strengthened its brand and those of its partners.

Be the Quote

The 2009 Video Music Awards had barely begun when country singer Taylor Swift was presented its "Best Female Video" award. Before she could finish her acceptance speech, rapper Kanye West jumped onstage, took the mic from her hands, and said, "Yo, Taylor, I'm really happy for you, and I'm going to let you finish, but Beyonce had one of the best videos of all time." Swift and the audience were stunned silent, so Kanye repeated himself, then returned the mic to Swift and went back to his seat. Then house band leader Wale awkwardly said, "You can't blame a man for speaking his mind," but the audience started to boo, so yes it could and yes it did. Even though Kanye turned to Twitter before the evening was out to declare that he had been misunderstood, his career took a bit of a hiatus as the blogosphere ripped him apart and music buyers paused for some reflection.

Sometimes truth gets communicated in an instant. Both fans and detractors felt like they'd gained insight into Kanye's personality and level of emotional maturity (or their preconceived notions were affirmed). No amount of subsequent spinning or dissection could change what people saw in that brief, apparently unplanned moment. The impact of his short spell onstage—his brand truth inherent in his quote—was too strong. He let slip out what he was truly thinking.

We see it happen all the time in politics, though perhaps not as overtly. Microphones are left on at the most inopportune times or simply ignored. In 1984, President Ronald Reagan famously quipped, while he believed a mic was turned off that, "My fellow Americans, I'm pleased to tell you today that I've signed legislation that will outlaw Russia forever. We begin bombing in five minutes." It's hard to believe that anybody was surprised that he'd think such a thing. In late 2011, Reuters reported that President Barack Obama and French President Nicholas Sarkozy were discussing Israeli Prime Minister Benjamin Netanyahu during a private conversation at a G20 summit … only a mic had been left on. Sarkozy called Netanyahu "a liar" and Obama replied: "You're tired of him. What about me? I have to deal with him every day." Beware the open microphone if you're a world leader. It is said of American politics that a gaffe can be defined as "a moment when a politician speaks the truth," and the definition regularly proves itself true around the world.

In the corporate world, gaffes have telegraphed truth in ways that no consciously constructed communication could have. When BP's clearly embattled and exhausted CEO Tony

Hayward toured the devastation his company had caused in the Gulf of Mexico in 2010 with a reporter and said, "There's no one who wants this over more than I do. I would like my life back," nobody was surprised by the sentiment but rather that he'd uttered the words that confirmed it. In 2007, Sir Richard Branson was giving an interview to London's *Telegraph* newspaper and offhandedly referenced his company's aging trains between London and Glasgow with two brutally simple words: "they're f–ked." Certainly this was not the positioning his crack public relations staff had constructed for him, but it clearly (and quickly) communicated what he truly thought of the situation.

These sorts of quotes add a new dimension to the saying, "a picture is worth a thousand words," in that often it takes that many words to deconstruct a static or moving image. Visuals are very effective in communicating blunt, broad emotions, but because of that they're also fairly generic and can be misunderstood. (Is a pout evidence of a profound emotion or intestinal gas?) Visuals are also external, in that they capture the exterior and construct a context for it that ends at the frame through which the camera works. Words are different; they're internally generated, as someone has to utter or write them instead of simply be seen by a lens, and their context is not the setting in which they were generated but rather the larger, deeper truths they might address. Quotes are Truth Turning Points that have the capacity of cutting through the clutter of competing information and touching people's core beliefs and understanding. We think this is part of the reason why text is still the most reliable and oft-used medium for communicating. In many instances, words speak louder, or at least more truthfully, than images.

It's also diametrically opposite to how marketers conceive of brand messages. We work hard to give messages a "voice" that is true to the brand versus any expectations of how a real person would talk. Here are five qualities of communicating by "being the quote" and, in doing so, communicating more truthfully:

- **Vernacular.** Quotes carry truth when they're spoken in the common language of conversation, not the words used to describe many brand positions. Whether a slip or declarative statement, quotes that sound like they were spoken by a normal human being are more truthful than those that are written by a committee (or purport to come via generic voices of brands).

- **Un-nuanced.** Truth is blunt, and arguments to the contrary are probably trying to make a number of truthful comments at the same time. A truthful quote is simple and direct, making a direct and unavoidable connection between speaker and topic that leaves nothing to interpretation. It's probably smarter to issue more frequent quotes than trying to weave complicated ideas in fewer statements.

- **Brief.** Twitter's 140-character limit has done much to change the way people communicate (and the jury is still out on whether all of it is particularly good), but one of the reasons it's so popular is because it forces people to make their points quickly. When viewed in the context of wanting to avoid too much nuance, perhaps this limitation is a useful guide to creating truthful quotes.

- **Surprising.** A truthful quote needs to surprise, whether by affirming something consumers already thought they knew (but never expected to hear), or in delivering some new information. People have been conditioned to expect the opposite, sadly, so the challenge is to construct quotes that communicate things that will make people stand up and say to themselves, "Wow."

People have been conditioned to expect the opposite, sadly, so the challenge is to construct quotes that communicate things that will make people stand up and say to themselves, "Wow."

- **Quotable.** Sounds like an obvious point, but most quotes aren't quotable whatsoever; when they are, they often add nothing to a news report or blog post other than to fill up space. Words need to be chosen that can be used in other contexts, which usually means relying on the four points above. If your company doesn't have something to say that's worth quoting, you should ask yourself why you are saying it.

Interrupt the Journey

"Everyone's a gamer" was EA UK Marketing Director Stuart Lang's reaction to our personal confession of frequent gaming, even though we couldn't look less like a classic computer games audience (we left our teenage geekdom behind a number of years ago).

EA is a global leader in the computer game industry and makes many of the computer games we have all heard of, and maybe even played, including *The Sims, FIFA Soccer, PGA Tour,* and *Need for Speed.* The marketing of the company has undergone a complete revolution over the last few years from packaged good producer to service provider. You used to go into an established retailer and buy the new version of an established game in a box. Now consumers can interact with and buy the product in any way they choose to—in a box at a store or online with friends via a gaming console or cell phone or computer. As Lang puts it, "We make the games available to customers where they want it, how they want to play it, with payment terms that make sense for them." Many of the brands have free-to-play components, via Facebook for instance. Micro-transactions are standard now. The marketing team has therefore shifted from focusing on launches alone to keeping the brands active throughout the product's life cycle.

In Lang's view it is digital that has changed everything:

> Digital is the big enabler, from both a distribution and a communication perspective. It's also demanded that marketing evolve. That old perception of marketing as something of a dark art with a bad reputation with practitioners seeking to confuse or blind the customer to the truth is old and out of date. You can't be successful long-term with a "fire and forget" philosophy and you can't be successful unless you're anything less than candid and honest in your communications—both are old school mentalities from another era. Today's audience is too aware and tuned in and too influential to subscribe to anything less than the truth. You have to listen and learn. And to demonstrate that you've done so. We're a service industry now. Those that deliver the most engaging content and the best customer service and experience will thrive; those that don't won't.

Having said this, launches in this marketplace can still be huge news and are highly anticipated by consumers. *Call of Duty*—a warfare game made by one of EA's competitors, Activision—had a new game out in November 2011. The retailers began advertising preorders in their windows in June 2011. It's hard to think of another installment of content that is so looked forward to in a mass-market way (unless, say, J.K. Rowling brought out an eighth Harry Potter novel).

It was to combat the earlier version of *Call of Duty* that EA's marketing team created a great TTP moment in the United Kingdom for the launch of EA's warfare game *Battlefield Bad Company 2* (*BFBC2*).

"The warfare genre is highly competitive," said the media agency's lead John Walsh. "*Call of Duty* had been the number-one [game] in the market and was dominating the landscape. EA's *Battlefield Bad Company 2* marketing budgets in the United Kingdom were like David versus Goliath in comparison."

The team decided that it should use warfare gaming tactics to "take *Call of Duty* down," as it was put to us. Essentially what it did was come up with a very new way to use an online search to interrupt the customer journey to get them to try and then buy the EA game instead of the market leader.

Most of the competitors in this market would have shied away (and did, actually) from competing head to head with *Call of Duty* by moving their activity outside of its key sales period. Walsh said EA decided to do the opposite and to take the market leader on, despite only having a quarter of its communications budget.

EA devised a new tactic to persuade customers of what they considered superior game play of *Battlefield Bad Company 2*.

Activision had created a YouTube channel for users to sample *Call of Duty* online. So EA set up a YouTube channel sampling *BFBC2*'s superior game play in videos that they knew would amaze and attract new users. Within the channel, consumers were given the opportunity to follow *BFBC2* on Twitter or to preorder the game immediately. Here's the really clever bit: YouTube had very recently released a keyword tool similar to Google with which you could bid for and purchase keywords. In this case it enabled EA to target people who typed in specific video searches on YouTube and serve their advertising for *BFBC2* to people who had come to YouTube to look for *Call of Duty*. Because it was new, it was generally underused by the advertising market and therefore a good value, as specific search terms were not costly to own. Better yet, no one in the gaming market had used it at all at this point in 2009. The team bought promoted video placements around all potential *Call of Duty* search terms. When the potential customers that Activision had attracted through its own marketing searched for samples of the game on YouTube, *BFBC2* was prominent among the video results returned. *BFBC2* openly and pointedly called customers to come and try their game instead. Not one penny was wasted as EA only paid for people who clicked through to try the *BFBC2* channel. The results were beyond expectations for such a low-risk strategy. Sales were nearly three times the budgeted expectations.

The EA *BFBC2* ambush of the customer journey showed the kind of predatory spirit that is of course rewarded in the game play itself. The team essentially raided the competition's marketing effort and, in martial arts fashion, turned the big player's apparent superior strength to EA's own advantage. It also represented another step on the journey for the marketing team of constantly step-changing the approach to consumers to ensure that they stay one step ahead of the competition, and in line with the consumers own media consumption. *Battlefield 3* now competes headlong with *Call of Duty* in the preorder charts and, at the time of this writing, it is well placed to take serious market share as a result of the work and learnings gathered from *BFBC2*'s campaign.

Stuart Lang's marketing approach overall is to be as transparent as possible with his consumers because word of mouth is paramount. "You can't get away with marketing spin anymore or with marketing as a dark art," he says. "Credibility is everything. You can't afford to blindside people and you have got to be seen as genuine." We couldn't agree more.

THE POSITIVE SIDE TO INTERRUPTION

The scientific field of "interruption science" looks at how human beings react to interruptions, and it turns out that there are at least two core facts that guide our responses:

1. We're genetically predisposed to perceive and react to changes in patterns, probably because it's how our ancestors were able to separate the sound or sight of predators from the hum of the forest.
2. We modern-day types might complain about distractions and the requirements of multitasking, but we rely on them to self-identify the exceptions that deserve our attention.

So we're built to react to interruptions and they're somewhat important to us, yet the accepted marketing canon these days is that interruptions are *bad*. Engagement, the focused attention part, is the desired *good*. It seems to us that a good interruption is preferable to a bad or pointless engagement, and that perhaps the problem with much of advertising in the recent past is that it squandered the attention it consciously and instinctively commanded.

Conclusion

Flashes of insight and understanding are common in books and movies. Great painters see their Mona Lisas. Composers hear the perfect melody in the whisper of the wind through the trees, or realize a rhythm by listening to the cadence of horses at gallop or the patter of rain on a windowsill. Inventors hit upon their discoveries sometimes despite looking in the wrong direction or pursuing a failed path of experimentation. Truth demands to be recognized, and this dramatic conceit is not without proof in real life. Many people report discovering what they were searching for less gradually and more instantly.

This difference between *deciding* and *knowing* is what we're calling a TTP, or "Truth Turning Point." They're moments that defy every convention on which we rely to teach and share; they aren't the conclusions of lengthy conversations or reasoned debate. *They just are*, in ways that activate our prior knowledge, intentions, and desires, and do so within a context that makes the experience immediately real.

We find no evidence that a brand can rely on orchestrating such instances alone—both because they're harder to invent in the first place, and every success makes it that much hard to top with another (there's no repeating)—but that they can provide an important complement to how your brand is perceived. It may help you to think of TTPs as devices or tools that you can use to immerse your content into the context of a moment of experience. It's a way of having conceptual shorthand, not in a symbolic, old-fashioned way, but in a digitally and immediate way. TTPs are moments of experience—of doing, touching, knowing—that are a core tool in the arsenal of brands that communicate truth.

There are likely many ways to craft TTPs. We've noted and dissected six in this chapter:

- Ignore the script
- Break the format
- Exceed the platform
- Expand the brief
- Be the quote
- Redirect a journey

There's risk that comes with each of these approaches, some more than others, because they all dare you to do things differently than you'd normally contemplate (and in ways that your consumers might not otherwise expect). That's the funny thing about truth, though: it comes out whether you want it to or not, so there's risk that truth will come out behind every campaign you consider. Whatever truth you don't address head-on has the possibility of emerging once the campaign is under way, only coming from a third party (that very well could have been your advocate or supporter on the front end). The closer and quicker you can get to truth right out of the gate, the easier it will be to defend and further your position.

You're in the truth-telling business, whether you do it actively or not.

TRUTH TURNING POINTS CHECKLIST

1. Have there been any recent Truth Turning Points for your category? What brands have delivered them, and what do you think they accomplished?

2. What's the biggest TTP surprise you could orchestrate for your brand in the shortest amount of planning time?

3. If you burn some bridges with an outrageous TTP, what is the worst that can happen? Could you be pleasantly surprised?

4. Is there a media owner that can help you to create a TTP with impact for your brand? Can a media owner help you to redirect a customer journey?

5. What measures should you put in place to ensure a bad TTP never happens? How could you preemptively deliver TTPs instead of waiting for your detractors or competitors to do it?

6. If you had to select a single image that delivered the most compelling truth about your brand, what would it be (and why)?

7. When you write copy for ads or for your website, how long does it take for you to explain your brand benefits? If you had a fifth of the space to use, could you describe the same truths?

8. Metaphor is a powerful communications tool, so how could you use it to deliver a truth about your brand? Could it be shorthand for you?

9. What would happen if you recalibrated your existing brand content across different platforms, swapping the stuff on one medium for that of another? How would it change the experience of your content? Would it reveal ways to deliver more truth, or perhaps ways to avoid missing it?

10. What was the simplest, most true thing you communicated about your brand over the past six months? What made it so, and why isn't everything you do equally compelling?

7

Use Point-of-Action Media

Today, everyone needs to be an expert at multi-tasking. Just think how hard you work to focus on a single thing, or the times that you're easily or repeatedly distracted when trying to do so. Pause for a moment and take stock of the sights, sounds, and thoughts that are vying for your attention right now; an irritating noise outside, some chore you need to get to before long, a song or thought that just won't leave you alone. Texts, emails, and tweets are a constant in the background, demanding that you master some fugue mental state of "ambient engagement" or "micro-interactions." Worse, whatever you're doing, you're also contemplating what you just did and will do next. All of us live in an endless narrative of moments in which we do many things at the same time, never or rarely just one thing. Our days are filled with layer upon layer of interruptions, thoughts, and competing requirements for our attention.

And marketers think anybody has the time or ability to get "engaged" with our conversations, let alone the desire?

No technology is immersive enough, and no creative content is compelling enough, to overcome the influences of place, time, and circumstance, yet many consumer conversations are created and maintained as if they benefited from rapt, full attention. Nothing could be further from the truth (pun intended).

How many times have you been driving with the radio on and heard and then promptly forgotten a phone number or website address? Have you had friends watching TV or a web video with you who added their running commentary to whatever was on the screen? Are there times that you see creative spots or Internet search results that have no apparent connection to what you were looking for at that particular time? Do your interests, patience, and willingness to learn change depending on your mood and circumstances? Of course they do.

The who, where, when, and why of consumer experience— the context of our busy, multitasking lives—influence our perceptions, engagement, and retention, sometimes more so than the what of conversations themselves. Creating meaningful conversations means understanding these "frames" that go around the "art" of marketing communications.

Yet most marketing is intended to rise above context, hence the idea that ads or online content should "break through the clutter" with creative that enables them to be memorable above all else. It has been this way since the first ads ran on radio in the early 1900s and it's true with today's latest and most egregiously silly or awful videos on YouTube. Context is something to be escaped or ignored. It's a cost of doing business.

Not only does this practice distract marketers from delivering truth, but ignoring the requirements and routines of context renders any real truths less believable.

We understand context as a great palette upon which to build meaningful and truthful conversations; in fact, addressing the exigencies of context allows smart marketers to establish more truthful (and thus more motivational and resilient) campaigns, making their marketing spends more efficient and effective. It's a core element of delivering truth that you cannot afford to overlook.

Our research has yielded six broad aspects to context—the contextual details of experience—that should appear on your radar screen as you develop your plans for consumer conversations:

1. **Consumption.** Relate consumption to how your messages will be used, not on eyeballs (i.e., audience demographics are less important than audience behaviors).

2. **Expectations.** Your expectations of retaining attention need to be matched to the purpose and value you offer.

3. **Environment.** Be aware of what else is going on when your message is being delivered, both as direct and indirect influences on consumption.

4. **Utility.** It is vitally important that you offer some sort of immediate utility.

5. **Socialness.** Your marketing communications is most usually experienced in groups, not alone, so you're talking to more than one person at a time.

6. **Continuity.** You need to recognize the larger "conversation" that is going on about your product or service, and see every marketing activity as a moment within this broader context.

We want to explore these six aspects of context in some detail, but first a starting ground rule: we're not talking about social media technology as the exclusive purview of conversation, because it's not. Effectively addressing context means seeing and understanding its role in every conversation between brands and consumers. Facebook doesn't own the idea, nor does Twitter (or whatever technology tool comes next); in fact, focusing exclusively on such platforms skews the conversation toward the mistaken presumption that people have focused interactions with their computer or smartphone screens.

Truth emerges from a multitude of experiential qualities, so let's take a novel approach to it and see how it emerges from a variety of conversations, both present and past.

Consumption: A Flight Less Fancy

It was 1993 and Don E. Schultz got a call from Lufthansa, the German national airline, asking for his help in finding the right media mix for its newest TV commercial.

You might have heard of Schultz because he essentially invented the idea of integrated marketing communications, or IMC. "I saw the need for a holistic approach to marketing communications, from data-driven research to media channel selection, long before we had the systems to accomplish the task," he explains. "I'm not sure if it was a gift or a curse, but by the mid-1980s we'd done enough work to see that the traditional media approach of 'buying eyeballs' wasn't going to survive: too much clutter, too little attention."

Lufthansa wanted Schultz to critique its spot, debuting its first wide-body Airbus 340 that was to be introduced on the United States–Germany route. So one morning, he hopped a train at New York's Penn Station and traveled to the company's headquarters on Long Island, NY. There he was met by the company's marketing leadership and led into a large boardroom to see the new commercial.

He remembers his reaction. "It was the airline version of the typical auto ad. The plane soaring in the blue sky, sun glinting on it with stirring music to fit. It was really pretty and I told them so."

Schultz was next shown a half-dozen media plans, each with a different approach to maximizing exposure to those perceived to be the demographically desirable Lufthansa passengers. When asked which plan he liked, Schultz immediately said, "None of the above."

The room fell silent until one of the Lufthansa execs asked him what they should do instead.

"I told them that they should skip TV entirely and show it on their airplanes," he recalls. "They already had customers squished in their narrow-body planes flying seven or eight hours on most transatlantic routes. So, the best prospects were the customers they already had. Those were the people that would really pay attention because the new plane solved one of their biggest problems—lack of space—which the A340 provided." He went on to conclude that other airlines would be launching the same wide-body planes soon, so Lufthansa needed to secure its existing customers before trolling for new ones.

The room was silent again, and then one of his hosts said, "We're paying you the big bucks to tell us that?" Before Schultz could answer, the exec added, "We should have known that. Thank you."

Schultz explains:

Typically in those days a commercial was created first and then people figured out who they were going to show it to. I can remember sitting in multiple agency pitches, dwelling on the creative, only to be told near the end that there wasn't time left for the media plan. We'd show a few overheads, toss out a few reach and frequency numbers, drop some big name media outlets and we were done.

Lufthansa had shot a spot with a clear image of who they wanted to reach, and the benefit of the product but simply hadn't thought out where, when, how, or why they could communicate with those people.

Schultz added, "To me, it made much more sense to start with the consumer and his or her context, rather than relying on the traditional model of coming up with a beautiful campaign and then finding the right audience to view it. It was simply letting the cart lead the horse. We knew this twenty years ago, but seem to have forgotten it since."

"To me, it made much more sense to start with the consumer and his or her context, rather than relying on the traditional model of coming up with a beautiful campaign and then finding the right audience to view it." —Don Schultz

Schultz's idea of the centrality of media consumption, which we think is context expressed as an active verb, drives his latest research on the efficacy of social media conversations and overall optimization of media plans. Schultz distills his approach into four core questions that brands should ask before initiating any marketing initiative:

1. Do you know what forms of media your target audience consumes? This means not only what they're exposed to but also what they use to reach and share decisions.
2. Which media sources do *they* think are the most important? Our measure of time as an indicator of preference probably isn't enough, as something like Internet use might decline due to more efficient manipulation.

3. What media forms are they using together, i.e., what combinations are used in multitasking? One media interaction might lead immediately to the next, derive from one just prior, or simply depend on one another simultaneously (like email and mobile).

4. What are the most important consumer sources of information within the relevant product category? Chances are the substance and experience of that media will dictate, in part, what you choose to put in your communication.

Schultz adds:

Today, communicating with customers is a hell of a lot more complicated than just finding or buying ads based on media distribution. In reality, matching messages and customers can be just as messy and unpredictably misleading as the perfection found in those dark boardrooms. Just like you shouldn't hatch your content and then shop for an audience, it's also a bad idea to play exclusively to the behavior of your consumers in social media. Actions like friending and forwarding are perceived to be absolute benefits for the brand, but they're not, at least no more than assuming great creative will generate its own audience, both are meaningless without one another. The real benefit is in integrating from the customer's view and then seeing how things come together.

Expectations: An Apple Not a Day

Now contrast the Lufthansa ad example from the 1990s with Apple's latest marketing. Much has been said and written about the computer company's miraculous branding, and there's no use arguing with a communications model that consistently delivers stunning sales successes and leads cutting-edge trends like cloud computing and new user interfaces.

However, most analyses of Apple focus on the look and feel of its marketing, as if the truth of its brand is expressed by its image. This belief has prompted competitors to import similar marketing creative for their own campaigns, like Microsoft did when it developed its "I'm a PC" idea in response to the hilarious "I'm a Mac" spots. Marketers like to talk about the associative and emotional qualities of brands as if they're truths that can be copied and customized by creative execution alone.

We think Apple's genius is as much about recognizing the importance of context in determining the what and how of content development and distribution. An example would be the stingy way in which Apple approaches its consumers. It only asks for their attention when it has something important or useful to say.

By doing so, one of the company's most significant—if unspoken—brand attributes is that *it doesn't waste your time*, which is created by the context of its communication as much as its content, and creates almost a quid pro quo understanding from consumers, stock analysts, or media critics that when Apple speaks, it's telling people things that matter. This runs contrary to the accepted wisdom that brands are supposed to provide a steady stream of content to the marketplace; in fact, we see a direct correlation between "frequency" of communicating and "credibility" of message, irrespective of content and, in this case, it's an inverse ratio. In other words, the more you talk, the less meaningful it's perceived to be no matter what you're saying.

Consider the contrast between Apple's and Microsoft's approaches to public relations: in 2009. Apple issued fifty-five press releases, for an annualized rate of a little more than 4.5 announcements each month. Microsoft's rate was thirty-four releases per month for a total of 408, or about 7.5 times

Apple's rate. Strip out the trade-only news and you still have Microsoft talking to consumers a whole lot more. Add in the efforts of publicists working with mainstream and social media outlets and the numbers skew even farther in Microsoft's direction, as Apple has no PR agency working for it and has been noticeably absent from participation in any social media campaigning (you can't follow Apple on Twitter, for instance).

Did Microsoft have more than seven times more meaningful things to say to the world as Apple?

Probably not. There's a case to be made that news releases are searchable online, so Microsoft is effectively contributing to its library of information by issuing so many press releases. There are likely people somewhere in the world who will at some time want to discover, say, the news bit about some company partnership to develop something or other, but the more important question to ask is whether a surfeit of announcements reduces the meaning of whatever those announcements reveal. Is there an objective disincentive to talking too much?

Because of its stinginess, the slightest hint that Apple will make a public statement is itself news, and the ability to truly warrant news coverage is a driver of its news-making aspirations. So, after many months of comments and complaints in chat rooms, blogs, and news articles about its unwillingness to run Adobe Flash on its devices, Apple chose to post a letter from Steve Jobs on its website. No additional commentary, no riffs via Tweets or blog posts. The company won't release traffic numbers, but we suspect a lot of people read the letter. The posting had far more meaning and resonance than the benefits of a more common multiplatform communications campaign.

A detailed review of Apple's past few years of media releases suggests a few rules for such an approach:

- **Focus on products or services, not process.** Apple makes sure that its consumer-facing announcements only describe things that face consumers versus throwing out

a lot of development or other items related to process.
Is it reasonable to expect that the rarer niche audiences
for such news can find it in other ways? This allows every
announcement to seem tangible and real.

- **Announce things in past tense, not promises.** Apple is renowned for announcing new products as close as possible
  to the day they can ship to consumers (and taking orders
  when shipping isn't immediate), which only further enhances the credibility and relevance of what it says. News
  about forward-looking plans leaks out mostly through its
  financial reporting, but it asks to intrude into the context
  of consumers' lives only when it has something to sell.

- **Skip the hyperbole.** The past record of Jobs' effusive
  quotes aside, news out of Apple continues to stay pretty
  much to the point. It doesn't describe itself as a "world-
  leading *somethingorother*" and since it's focused on the
  here-and-now, it somewhat limits the purview of its content. So when an Apple story appears in your RSS feed,
  you can reasonably expect that it isn't full of blather.

Combining less frequent announcements with more substantive content appears to contribute significant meaning
to Apple's brand. Again, this observation runs counter to the
recommendations of most social media experts these days;
the conventional wisdom is to talk early and often, to para-
phrase the advice once given to Chicago voters. Since technology gives marketers visibility into all of the conversations
that have been going on between consumers since time began
(both inconsequential and occasionally important), the idea
is that brands need to submit content to these contexts.

Apple contributes, sure enough, but what it contributes has
meaning, and its communications process is a key enabler of
it. By building a sense of anticipation for its announcements,
it prompts the very interest in its brand that other businesses

try to buy through incessant conversation, and it makes whatever it chooses to say seem somehow more true. Any brand can try to follow Apple's marketing model and replicate its look and feel to no success whatsoever. Any brand could similarly succeed by understanding and respecting consumer expectations for time and attention.

Environment: Marketing That Warms Your Heart

Another way in which context matters is when you consider the direct and indirect influences on consumers' ability (let alone willingness) to care about what you want to say. Your message must address these influences to have meaning.

A good example of this quality could be found on a cold and blustery Chicago day in December 2008, when Kraft's Stove Top brand of meat stuffing chose to add heaters to ten outdoor bus stops. A giant ad inside the shelters declared "Warmth. Provided By Us," a giant picture of a steaming hot dish of the product, and some supporting text underneath. Experts call such campaigns "experiential marketing," but we see something more going on: it's vitally important to not simply offer experiences that evidence your brand but to acknowledge and support the experiences into which you presume to insert your brand messaging.

Getting warm on a cold day isn't a complicated idea. It's not a subtle benefit, either, nor does promising warmth require much, if any, deconstruction. In a world of nuanced communications, the prospect of being warm instead of cold constitutes a simple truth. It has meaning irrespective of who or what presents it. So the prospect of a warm bus shelter on a cold day meant something to Chicago commuters. It was the right message in the right context pretty much out of the box (or in it, as it were).

The connection to Stove Top was doubly smart because it related to its functional benefit of being a warm, toasty filler for dinnertime meals. The connection was simple and direct. Yet the primary strength of the strategy had less to do with the brand than with the context. It's inventors at Draftfcb and JCDeveaux waxed poetic about how the shelter and food were both warm, ergo the branding benefit, but any product or service could have supported the heaters and benefited from them. Now, warmth brought to you by Crystal Light Iced Tea might not make sense, but the point here is that the meaning for the consumer arose from the context and not initially, necessarily, or wholly from the branding message.

It also worked because the structure and delivery of the marketing conversation respected the other environmental qualities of the experience. For instance, think about how many people walk the streets today wearing MP3 player earbuds. Now consider how many are holding a mobile phone to the ears. The Stove Top conversation didn't require those otherwise occupied senses to come to bear on its messaging. Ditto for movement; consumers didn't have to stop in order to contemplate the message, although we're sure they were happy to linger under the heat lamps.

The total cost for the shelter campaign was approximately one hundred thousand dollars (according to *Promo* magazine), and it helped drive a 7 percent increase in sales volume over the same time period the year prior. Publicity coverage alone was estimated at 37.2 million media impressions, proving that acknowledging the environmental circumstances of context that influence consumer experience is an important and potentially lucrative area to explore.

There are many other examples that suggest that the consumption environment should guide your content development (and thus the efficacy of your meaning).

Utility: Hungry for the Sale

"Use it or lose it" is a popular dare, and it's immensely relevant to delivering meaningful communications. Today's consumer is busy and distracted so the days of extended stories or complicated jokes are long gone. We're not advocating blunt or crude messaging as much as clear and motivational messages. Utility in particular contexts is often far more meaningful than trying to insert meaning into *any* circumstance. Pick your shots.

We saw this in London in the mid-1990s, when Nick Lawson, now EMEA CEO of MediaCom, was asked to develop a pitch for Ovaltine. The brand's typical TV ad depicted a housewife rushing from one task to another, stopping to take a break now and then for refreshment. Lawson's great insight was to plot that real-life journey throughout the day and then correlate it with media habits. In other words, insert Ovaltine's marketing message into the real moments when its target housewives would not only want to, but be able to, consume its products.

The would-be client hated it and the team lost the pitch, but was either too smart or too young to give up on the concept. Their managing director, Steve Allan (now global CEO of MediaCom), has always believed that everything can and should be challenged. Skip forward a few years, add an even younger staffer named Steve Gladdis, and the agency tried a similar approach for another client.

Gladdis worked on the Roche account and a product called Rennie, which was an indigestion remedy. The agency's thinking for the client paralleled insights for most clients during that time, which meant trying to minimize the number of heavy TV viewers exposed to the ads, and increase the number of light viewers (who were harder to reach and therefore worth more to brands). The work pleased the client, but it made not the slightest impact on Rennie's actual sales.

Then one afternoon, as he was heading home from a client meeting, Gladdis was overwhelmed by the smell of shredded wheat from the Nabisco factory nearby. Suddenly he realized that he was also very hungry.

"Indigestion remedies are really boring products," said Gladdis. "I bet there is only one time when anyone is even remotely drawn to thinking about them and that is when they have just eaten too much and are feeling a bit queasy." So he set out to prove to Rennie that he could make the same TV advertisement work harder by putting it in front of the target audience in the right place and at the right time.

For the first time ever, a media agency bought the Family Food Panel, a quantitative research panel that measured what food was eaten throughout the United Kingdom and when and where. The data were a revelation: it is all common sense if you think about it, but the main meals of the day differ not only in name throughout the United Kingdom but they also don't take place at the same time either, running later, for instance, in areas where commuting time is long and difficult. In other cases, consumers in some areas pop home for a sandwich at lunchtime.

Gladdis and his colleagues set about mapping this data and producing a dramatically different airtime buying strategy. Nearly all of the airtime was bought within two hours of eating—what they called the "Point of Suffering." The sales results exceeded even Gladdis's wildest hopes: after nine months of implementation, the like-for-like sales were up 12 percent.

Rennie remains the purest version of the idea simply because it was only a media planning and buying strategy. The content remained unchanged. Understanding the context in which an ad is being seen is a key way to make the communications more effective. Whenever advertising is placed we should ask not just how many of the audience is being reached but also what evidence we can find about their frame of mind.

Socialness: So Obvious a Gorilla Couldn't Do It

We are consistently struck by how the revolution in social media technologies has changed how we need to look at *all* media interactions. There have been conversations going on since Sears printed its first catalogue in the 1800s up through Twitter's coverage of the Iranian elections of 2009. We marketers just never saw things that way. What happened before and after our advertising or general marketing was somehow beyond our purview, or quite literally not on our radar. This meant that the role of *groups* in making decisions was not always a top priority.

It's surprising to us how much commercial speech today still doesn't acknowledge this reality beyond the give-and-take on social media sites. Conversation started long before Facebook and goes on far beyond it, and it's up to smart marketers to address and add meaning to it. All media contributes to the conversation. Let's look at the United Kingdom's Galaxy chocolate to illustrate this point.

People in the United Kingdom grow up with a choice between two iconic chocolates, just like Americans choose between Coke and Pepsi. Cadbury and Galaxy are both iconic, especially with women. Galaxy is often preferred in blind taste tests, but Cadbury is a famous British heritage brand that often overshadows its rival.

In recent years Cadbury has done lots of celebrated advertising for its brand, such as using new media to distribute a video of a gorilla drumming in front of a backdrop evoking the purple of its packaging. No mention of chocolate or any meaning other than the clutter-busting image of a gorilla rocking to a Genesis song. It followed that with a video of airport equipment doing some sort of close-order drill. Again, no meaning inherent or obvious, but lots to talk about.

Galaxy chose a different path by electing to contribute meaning to the group/conversational activities and thereby drive product preference. Its first decision was to ignore nearly half of the consumers who buy its products.

A deep investigation revealed massive differences between the ways men and women bought Galaxy chocolates, even though they purchased them in nearly equal numbers. Women love thinking, talking, anticipating, and dreaming about chocolate, while men buy it on impulse and find little meaning in doing so. So there was a potential role for groups within the buying context for women and not one for men. Women take chocolate seriously.

Women love thinking, talking, antici-pating, and dreaming about chocolate, while men buy it on impulse and find little meaning in doing so.

The communications platform the team developed was expressed as "Galaxy—Your accomplice in indulgence," and it was intended to demonstrate to women through every element of an integrated campaign that Galaxy understood what they meant by indulgence better than any other brand. After considering associations with shopping and girly movies, the team landed on a somewhat surprising context: reading, truly, was self-indulgence.

The initial idea became an all-encompassing ownership of a core feminine contextual moment. The Galaxy "Irresistible Reads" promotion was created, in which every buyer of a chocolate bar had the chance to win a free book. One million books later this was Galaxy's biggest ever promotion. All the books were Galaxy branded and contained Galaxy book-marks, which meant that the branding would be lasting as people lent the books and reused the bookmarks—in effect creating a new medium as Galaxy's very own, and uniquely owned materials were carried in handbags, rested on bedside tables, and passed around among friends.

This went far beyond the confines of typical sponsorship, however. Galaxy not only sponsored TV's *Richard and Judy* book club segment (The United Kingdom's version of Oprah's Book Club) but followed it with partnerships with supermar-kets. For example, Asda had its own book club in association with Galaxy that created stand-alone and new display stands outside of the confectionary sections. New distribution outlets were also generated as Galaxy began promoting the branded book club in bookshops where chocolate had never been sold before. And the brand thrived on this unique contextual planning. The company also created the Galaxy British Book Awards, the only book award that gives the public a say in the selection of the winner.

Acknowledging the role of context and community in ef-fectively communicating the truth reaped great rewards for Galaxy. As one pundit said, "Cadbury may have grabbed all the headlines with its award-winning 'Gorilla' ad, but its arch-rival Galaxy has been stealing the hearts of UK consumers. The Mars brand clinched the top spot in the chocolate sector with this very different marketing strategy" (*Marketing Magazine,* "Most Loved Brands," Survey 2007).

Continuity: Before and After

While Galaxy so effectively mobilized the context of commu-nity interaction, there's also the importance of recognizing the broad conversations under way in society that might influence the meaning consumers derive from your marketing communications. A good example of this would be to look at the car industry.

We would all agree that the worldwide automobile business has undergone massive change, and that nobody is going to buy a car tomorrow in the same way, or for the same reasons, as they did in the past. Issues of environmental impact, safety, country of origin and, of course, the overall economy and vehicle purchase costs are combining in new and unique ways to influence sales.

In other words, there's a "conversation" going on about cars, and it's one that car marketers need to address. Many brands have contributed product information (such as the all-electric Nissan Leaf or the hybrid-electric Chevy Volt) and social chatter (like the Ford Fiesta Movement, which put twentysomethings in cars so they could blog about the vehicle, and themselves). Hyundai is an intriguing example of how to create meaning by reaching past the obvious handles for messaging and instead adding needed truth to a broader conversation.

During the peak of the recent economic woes, Hyundai centered its marketing on offers: first, it said it would let people return their purchases if they lost their jobs within a few months of buying, and second, it let owners hedge the price they were willing to pay for gas. Both of these offers had immense meaning because they addressed the conversation that consumers were having *before* they got around to buying a car (our economic world is collapsing) and they applied to the world *after* any conversation about buying a car (what if the economic world is still collapsing).

In this case, the medium of these communications was far less important than the content. Ads are arguably not "social" when there's no content in them worth talking about but they certainly make sense when there is. Ditto goes for any other media. The reverse is also true: definitively "social" media conversations with nothing worthwhile fed into them have no meaning. What Hyundai chose to do was address the substance of conversation that would influence any direct conversation it might want to have with customers, and incorporated it therein. It makes fuel-efficient, lower-priced, reasonably reliable vehicles, but it realized that those benefits weren't enough. They had no meaning unless the broader conversation was addressed first. Context mattered.

The result? Hyundai's market share almost doubled, and the little-known brand got on many people's buying lists during a time when sales of most other brands were flat or down. The marketer behind the strategy was then recruited by GM to try and work the same magic there.

There are other examples of this quality of context. Contrast Microsoft and Domino's, for instance. Microsoft introduced Windows 7 without even obliquely referencing the shortcomings of its previous operating system, Vista, yet the memory of that earlier product's shortcomings (not to mention ownership of it) was certainly vivid for many. Conversely, Domino's ran a campaign in 2009 that explicitly admitted that its pizza tasted terrible and that the company had improved it. Did it taste worse than Vista frustrated its product owners? There's no way to tell, but we think the sales successes of Domino's—a "historic" leap of 14.3 percent during the quarter immediately following the campaign—suggest a productivity for its marketing that Microsoft would love to see for its own spending.

The idea of providing meaning in the ongoing conversations around us seems dependent on how we define those conversations, and the broader and more explicit we make the connections—and populate them with truth—the more meaningful the result.

MAKING FUNNY PAY

Many of the most memorable ads or commercials are funny, even though humor has never been directly correlated with selling anything. A good laugh is a great way to gain attention within a variety of contexts, but here's a good test: challenge yourself to recollect a spot that made you laugh over the past year, and then try to remember the product or service it presumed to promote; chances are you can't and, even if you do, you probably can't make the connection between your chuckles and a subsequent sample, purchase, or reuse. Funny just isn't a brand attribute (any more than sex appeal, but that's another story).

When does funny work? When it's tied to a functional benefit, so it makes sense in the context of its experience and thus becomes memorable for something more. In this way, it can be a tool for communicating truth. Consider the GEICO insurance mascot, which is probably recognizable to every conscious American consumer these days. Does the humor mean anything? Is insurance supposed to be funny, or do you trust a provider that presents one of its key executives as a CGI lizard? No, what's meaningful in this strategy is the line, "Fifteen minutes could save you 15 percent or more on your car insurance." This messaging emerges from the funny context and can live on to drive subsequent consumer inquiries. No thought or translation is required. It's an elegantly simple declaration.

Another example would be the Ally TV campaign we discussed earlier, in which a smarmy bank executive

(continued on next page)

makes a little kid talk to a windup doll that can't understand her request to play with toys. It's hilarious, but it's also meaningful because there's a punch line at the end promising that customers will "always get a live person" when they call the bank. The joke resonates with the pitch, enhancing its meaning instead of detracting from it (or being utterly irrelevant). You "get" it.

Funny has no intrinsic truthfulness, but the truth can be funny.

Conclusion

Understanding that truth arises from the influences of context as much as, if not more than, your stated or implied messaging is a paradigm-shifting realization, because it means how you identify, analyze, and construct your presence *within* said contexts should drive the content, whether creative or functional (like votes, links, or other behavioral mechanisms).

This element of being truthful applies to all media, whether digital or analog, and is also irrespective of any specific definition of context or "place." Context has dimensions of space, time, and human behavior, which means that your conversations span multiple avenues. There are three fundamental qualities of context that you need to consider:

1. **It's media neutral.** Of course the qualities of the mediated experience must be understood and addressed, but there are many more inputs into any context. The idea that you can have a "digital strategy" neglects to consider the many analog qualities of any digital media experience (human experience occurs in a noisy and conflicted

reality that is anything but digital). Further, many of the latest delineations between "social" and other media are distractions when every context has a social element; some are better recognized and addressed than others. Media are tools to become part of experiential contexts, but they don't constitute the contexts themselves.

2. **It's biased.** Conclusions and outcomes of experience emerge from a combination of preconceived notions and the experiences themselves, which meld to create unique, somewhat unrepeatable moments. There's a bias to these moments—consumer conclusions and subsequent actions will be decided by a combination of factors and not necessarily your inputs—so the challenge is to address this while keeping your communications strategy in mind. Being present in various places isn't synonymous with successfully saying or accomplishing anything.

3. **It's unforgiving.** Meaning is a fickle, somewhat transitory phenomenon: a fact can resonate with meaning in one context and seem utterly foolhardy in another. Something that has meaning with an audience one time might be rendered meaningless if repeated too often or without change. So it's important to understand the levers for meaning available to you in any context, and then address them accordingly. Meaning isn't additive as much as real time, so if you can't be reasonably sure a certain context enables you to deliver meaning, you might reconsider your presence in that setting. Addressing context might include learning to stop while you're ahead.

POINT-OF-ACTION MEDIA CHECKLIST

1. When is the consumer most open to hearing from you? Is there a format that is most appropriate at that point, and how does that form affect what you're able to communicate?

2. Can you correlate the most opportune moment to communicate with the best media through which to accomplish it, and then own it for your category?

3. What are the points during the consumer journey where you might lose them? How can you make sure you strengthen the truths you communicate at those moments?

4. What aspects of your marketing budget have no immediate response attached to them (other than an emotional or retentive one)? Why?

5. Would there be a downside if you overcommitted to the best point-of-action media moment?

6. Reaching a conclusion quickly and unequivocally makes it easier to take subsequent action (the setup is faster and more compelling), so how could you focus more of your media on action points instead of lengthy exposition?

7. Consider what each medium can deliver for your customer journey. How could you use a billboard to deliver an actionable truth about your brand? What about radio?

8. Consider your most comprehensive list of leads and would-be customers and what you might ask them to do instead of consume or ponder.

9. What did you tell your consumers today that they *needed* to know in order to buy your brand, instead of what you *wanted* them to know?

10. If you stopped calling people who'd bought from you more than three months ago "customers" and instead recognized them for what they were—effectively "strangers"—what prompt would you share with them next?

8

Leverage Routine

Here's a thought experiment for you—Take stock of your day, whether retroactively if you're reading this in the evening or proactively if you're grabbing a few pages before starting for work or play. Consider putting your activities into two categories: The first is labeled "Norms," and put into it all the things you're going to do (or did) today that you do every day, generally speaking. The second, entitled "Exceptions," are the activities that stand out as somehow notable or different. Ready? Sit back and give it a minute or two. We'll see you at the start of the next paragraph.

Welcome back. Here's our guess at what you discovered:

- **Norms.** This is the longer list, even though it's harder to decide what merits getting onto it, right? You do dozens, if not hundreds of things every day without expending much psychic or intellectual capital. They're the things you chose to do at one point, or felt compelled to do, so in this sense they're internally driven. Your norms are the habits and routines that define the ebb and flow of your daily experience, even if they do so somewhat unconsciously.

- **Exceptions.** This is a much shorter list that is mostly circumstantial, in that exceptions are mostly the external effects that disrupt or change your normal routines. They stand out whether for good or bad reasons, however, and they're memorable more in terms of the intensity of the exception than its other qualities. They're also consciously apparent to you, insomuch as you have no real expectation that tomorrow will repeat any of them. If it did, today's exceptions would be on their way to becoming norms.

Most brand experiences are norms, not exceptions. You use products and avail yourself of services without expending much conscious involvement to determine whether you'll use that bar of soap in the shower, put on the shirt in your closet, or drink the coffee or tea from the nearest pot. Your habits and routines dictate this consumption, this brand engagement, and the fact that most of your involvement is on autopilot means you have room in your day to be involved with many different brands. If you had to contemplate the effects of different shampoos every time you reached for a bottle in the shower or walked down the aisle of your grocery store, you'd get little done. Brands are therefore the shorthand that labels your prior decisions.

Exceptions are impromptu new decision points. The most common prompts are when products or services fail or fall short of expectations. A routine is interrupted, a habit broken, or a new need arises for which there's no obvious or immediate solution. It's at these moments that consumers are literally forced to get consciously engaged with brands, and it's at these times that brands hope to reaffirm loyalty or steal it from a competitor. This is why online customer complaints get so much attention from marketers these days; not only are they the exceptions at which brand preferences could change for better or worse but social sharing means that one consumer's exception could shake others out of their routines. Customer service has been recast as a process of managing exceptions, really, in that service, like functional performance, is a quality of the ongoing routines on which consumers rely. What causes the exceptions to those habits are service failures or shortcomings. Today's customer service is really "routine fixing," or "habit acquiring."

The other source for exceptions is when brands proactively choose to ask for their consumers' conscious engagement in order to experience or examine an improvement or new benefit. Innovations drive these exceptions. Retailers send notice of a new price promotion. Ads run declaring increased surfactants in dishwashing liquid, or better perspiration protection in an underarm deodorant. There's a new giveaway or event warranting more friending behaviors on a social site. Like problems, these exceptions are seen as chances to reaffirm customer loyalty or attract new customers, so traditional branding thinking is that they should be sought after. Innovation is the tool that can force positive brand engagement.

We'd like to make the case for the norm—the ongoing provision of satisfying experiences—as an unsung hero of branding, primarily because it's the substance of brand truth and providing it is the mechanism for doing it.

The context of experience is less moment and more process or duration of time. Exceptions are certainly events that can reaffirm or deny truth, but it's the ongoing behavior of companies and the performance of their products or services that establish and support truth in the first place. Just think back to your mental list from the start of this chapter, and ask yourself if a stellar customer service moment or brilliant product innovation could change what you know to be true about a brand. It can't overcome the negative truth of your ongoing experience unless there are a repeated and regular series of them, at which point they become the norm. If you're a would-be customer, the event can warrant your attention but a simple Internet search will let you know if the exception is truly exceptional or an expression of routine. Either way, the norm is what's true, not the exception.

Truth is regularly a routine, not necessarily an occasional realization.

It works better when it fits into existing routines versus being used as a tool to create new ones. The repeatable, reliable context of truth has significant implications for the questions you ask about how you deliver your marketing communications:

- **Promises.** Is the goal of your brief to get consumers to think things (old or new) about your brand, or do you want to ask them to consider their own routines? Is your positioning a statement of an exception or a declaration of a norm? It might not seem obviously sexy to promote a habit, but overcoming that creative challenge might make whatever you're saying more truthful. Asking a consumer to do something is a binary decision—she or he can conclude "yes" or "no"—versus the myriad interpretations that are required by statements of ideas.

- **Delivery.** *Education* is one of the worst words ever applied to brand or marketing strategy, at least from the perspective of delivering truth. Even though consumers are very capable of learning, it is nearly impossible for brands to teach; the conversation just doesn't work that way, and when marketers approach distribution channels in search of media that can afford them the space to educate (either available real estate and/or duration of time), it's usually evidence of an inability to distill the truth in what they want to say. A smarter approach might be to consider media in terms of how close they are to consumers using information in their lives (see point above). Attach your delivery to what they already know (and do).

- **Support.** If routine is the unsung hero of brand awareness, then customer service is its misperceived minion. We tend to view it as the mechanism of exceptions (it has driven much theory and expenditure chasing problems online, for instance), when it could be seen as the tool for maintaining habits and thereby supporting the truth of brand promises and delivery. Subscriptions, auto-renewals, updates and upgrades, and other actions that are categorized as operational activities could be elevated to strategic efforts to support routines. The very way these benefits are delivered speak to habits and should be exploited, not assuming to be tangential to the marketing strategy overall.

The truth of your brand isn't determined by how many unsatisfied customers you help but by how many satisfied customers rely on your products or services. The context for encouraging, delivering, and supporting these behaviors is a tool for communicating truth. Do truth regularly and often, from your strategies to the slightest executional tactics. We've collected business cases to illustrate the various ways you can apply this thinking to your work.

Twix and the Tea Lady

The concept of "Tea Ladies" is a uniquely British custom dating
back to World War II, when morale in the United Kingdom
was low and the government needed work production to be
higher, so women were hired with the sole job of making the
office and factory rounds at tea time and providing a nice cup
of tea, piece of cake, or a bun (thus simultaneously cheering
workers and keeping them at the jobs). This idea built on a
national tradition of drinking tea that dated back to the nine-
teenth century. Tea ladies became a much-loved institution
through cameo performances in a number of enduring British
comedy TV shows and movies in the 1950s, well past the war
years, even though the next generation of people hadn't experienced the delights of the tea round, in part because the tea
ladies' jobs had been made redundant as vending machines
in the workplace took over. Of course, a vending machine
doesn't chat with you or know your name and can't tell if you
look under the weather and need cheering up, so tea ladies
were preserved as an icon that has continued to be an easily
recognizable reference to a rather invented but nonetheless
nostalgic Golden Age of the late 1940s and 1950s. Tea ladies
were a routine long before iced cinnamon lattes and skinny
cappuccinos frequented our consciousness.

The tea breaks that Britain's tea ladies came to symbolize
are more than an idea or stereotype, however. The British love
taking their tea, and doing so carries with it an almost instinc-
tive sense of pause and relief. So while national stereotyping is
something that we all lapse into occasionally—French women
never get fat, Italian men are all flirtatious, Americans are too
loud—the idea of taking a break for tea is a largely flattering,
charming, and benign habit. That the Brit would drop everything to have a cup of tea religiously at 4 p.m. daily is a cul-
tural meme that just won't go away.

That's because it's true. How it became true for Twix is an interesting example of marketing to routines, not exceptions. Twix is a chocolate bar that was in everyone's top five chocolate bar choices, but in 2008 wasn't on top of enough people's lists. Although a huge seller in Britain with a well-known profile, since it wasn't the favorite, its rate of sale was below expectations for what was possible in the category. Most people thought of it bracketed with its major competitor Kit Kat, which had been marketing to routines for decades with its "Have a break, have a Kit Kat" slogan. Twix had had changing ad strategies as creative agencies tried to give it meaning for a variety of target audiences through thirty-second TV spots. Those efforts had not generated the hoped-for sales uplift, yet the team still had high ambitions for the bar.

"What is Twix good for?" asked Matt Mee, one of the brand's agency team members at one of many meetings intended to find a compelling and regular purpose for consuming Twix. With the help of the team's own experience with the candy bar and a lot of consumer insight, the answer came back fairly quickly and somewhat obviously: truthfully, Twix was the perfect complement to a cup of tea. In fact, Mee's team of Andy Walsh, Louise Martell, and Oli Seares found evidence that some people even suck their tea through a Twix like a straw (and yes, of course, there is now a Facebook page for those consumers so inclined).

Tea truly is a national institution in the United Kingdom, despite there being coffee shops everywhere. Scratch the surface of many Brits and you will find them wanting or even needing a nice cup of tea regularly through the day, the lack of which being the main complaint they'll make about going abroad for a holiday in Paris, Las Vegas, Venice, or the Azores. According to the UK Tea Council, the tea break has been an institution for more than two hundred years. Today in the United Kingdom, 165 million cups of tea will be drunk.

If tea and Twix would be a natural match, the next step was to find a way to make a solid association between the brand and the routine. The strategic team concluded that the first, second, or even third step on this journey would not be through advertising. The connection was not something that could be declared. There might be an advertising solution, but it would not lead the communications. Instead of pursuing a creative concept to embody the strategy, the team created a series of partnerships, sponsorships, and promotions that prompted action. The activities included sampling partnerships with teabag brands and getting a free "cuppa" with your Twix via an on-pack promotion (giving consumers a cup of tea at cafés and supermarkets throughout the United Kingdom along with their Twix).

A partnership with the United Kingdom's biggest daily tabloid newspaper, *The Sun*, set out to revive a much lamented British institution: the Tea Lady.

With a recessionary mood hitting Britain, it felt like perfect timing to bring her back. A contest intended to find her attracted entrants from all around the United Kingdom; the eventual winner embarked on a charity tea tour, from Land's End to John o' Groats, on a bicycle (setting a world record). Of course, she was tied in with a sampling tour, delivering tea and Twix to the nation.

Twix and tea breaks. The various campaign activities not only made the connection tangibly real but were successful in edging Twix into consumers' routines. There was significant sales growth and Twix became one of the hero brands within the portfolio. The basic truth about the brand—for a significant number of consumers it is better than other snacks for perfectly accompanying a cup of tea—was the insight on which the entire campaign was built. The strategy worked because it demonstrated and promoted the routine instead of simply declaring it. In essence, the job of the team was simply to allow this truth to come out, and not obfuscate it with too much up-front branding brilliance.

"If we'd started with just advertising, it wouldn't have worked," explained Walsh, MediaCom's media planner on the Twix account. "You have to create a community, start a network, deliver owned assets, establish and address routines, because that's about the truth of what we were claiming. Without this truth at the heart of it, the campaign wouldn't have worked."

Making the Microscopic Visible

Do you remember the days when you didn't think about washing your hands frequently during the day? We were all taught to do so after using the toilet and before eating, but otherwise the prohibitions were mostly reserved for the particularly or chronically hygienic among us. That all changed in 1997, when GOJO Industries introduced Purell hand sanitizer to the American market.

First, here's a little background on GOJO. The company was created after World War II by Goldie and Jerry Lippman to create and market a hand cleaner that was strong enough to remove the sort of gunk that Goldie used to get on her hands while working in a rubber factory during the war. In typical bootstrap fashion, the couple sold bottles from the back of Jerry's car, and soon learned that one of the primary consumer targets—automotive garages, with their repeat and regular hand-washing needs—felt the product was too expensive. A little digging revealed that they were using far too much of the fluid, which led the Lippmans to create the first portion-control hand cleaner dispenser, for which GOJO received a patent in 1952. (Contrast that innovation with other brands' interest in making cups and toothpaste tube openings larger than necessary to encourage overuse.)

The portion-dispensing approach led GOJO to new markets like health care and food service, where both employees and customers found themselves using soap that promised to have been "sanitary sealed" and apportioned for their unique use. It then built a commercial washroom business on these user benefits, which was supported by increased institutional attention to the dangers of hand-borne germs. These accomplishments all but preordained the company's invention of Purell, which was conceptually based on the idea that workers in so many occupations had regular cleansing needs, so why didn't consumers overall? Purell freed its sanitizing product from the limitations of place and water while promoting the idea that people could clean their hands at any point during their days. Nobody had conceived of washing their hands as they walked through doorways or checked inside their purses, yet everyone would consider it thereafter (and many make it a routine).

The branding relied almost completely on promoting a clearer understanding of the contexts in which the product could be used. An early ad from its agency (Wyse) read, "The average office desk has four hundred times more germs than a toilet seat. Bet you didn't get that memo." A campaign in Canada put stickers on magazines in doctors' office waiting rooms and then life-sized images on the insides of bathroom doors that read, "Caution: 92 percent of guys said they washed, 34 percent were lying," or, "You washed. This guy didn't." Artsy print ads in Australia showed hands marked or smudged by a variety of things (many of them yucky) with the tagline "You are what you touch."

Did traditional brand associations emerge from this marketing? We'd suggest not, but rather that consumers were made aware of a need, and turned to Purell less out of an affinity for the product and more because they felt compelled to start a new routine. They bought into the "idea" of hand sanitizing, which served Purell wonderfully in the early years but then made things more challenging for it once competitors appeared. It literally created a new market and then found itself fighting for market share, though things like the swine flu scare in 2009 helped grow the entire category by a whopping 70 percent.

The consumer business was a direct extension of GOJO's institutional business; the company was (and is) all about catering to routine uses, not impulse purchases or actions. In this way it has sold and built brands for more than half a century.

Today's Forecast Is for Fashionable Protection

Sometimes we don't want to hear the truth, even when we recognize its inevitability. This happens when we run away from listening to news stories, when the bleakness of just what is going on in the world is too much for us. It also happens every time a smoker takes out another cigarette or turns the pack over to avoid the health warning.

Cancer Research UK (CRUK) is the world's leading charity dedicated to beating cancer through research. The roots of the organization are more than a hundred years old, dating back to 1902, when the Royal College of Surgeons and Physicians set up the United Kingdom's first specialist cancer research organization. Back then, cancer wasn't the main cause of death; more people died from typhus, measles, and smallpox. But as treatments or immunizations against those diseases were found, life expectancies increased and exposed more people to the risks of developing cancer. Now, one in three can expect to be diagnosed in the United States and United Kingdom, though rates vary based on gender, genetics, and lifestyle.

Skin cancer is the second most common cancer among young adults (the fifteen to thirty-five age group). Sunburn when you are young increases the risk of skin cancer in later life. Most parents are now used to covering their kids up and slathering them with sunscreen, at least until the kids start thinking that they're the center of the universe and immortal. CRUK issued its first warning linking overexposure to the sun to skin cancer back in 1935, but current habits prove that providing the facts wasn't enough. Everyone in the target market was very good at ignoring things they didn't want to hear, particularly in an often cloudy country where having a suntan is inextricably linked to looking attractive. The United Kingdom has no taboo around tanning, or the burning that is the more common outcome for Anglo-Saxon skin types and often seen as part of the process of getting a healthy-looking tan. When the sun does come out in the United Kingdom, everyone immediately rushes out into it, strips off as much as possible and, if they're old enough, grabs a beer. There is no way a sensible message about spending time in the shade, let alone on a hot day, was ever going to have any sway with the young adults in this audience.

So in the summer of 2010, CRUK decided to tackle the problem in a new way, and introduce a new habit to go along with the routine.

If young adults are united in their disinterest in health warnings, they are, in large numbers, very interested in what to wear. They are at the height of experimentation with their looks. Behavior research revealed clear insights that appearance was the place to which it might be possible to introduce new habits since, perhaps not surprisingly, this audience doesn't think about whether what they're planning to wear increases or decreases the risk from overexposure to the sun. Hence was born CRUK's SunSmart fashion campaign.

Asos is one of the fastest growing and leading online fashion retailers. Established in 2000 and now the largest independent UK fashion site, Asos has always been more than just a fashion outlet, offering advice on what to wear and how to recreate a look seen on a favorite celebrity. The growth in women's fashion retailing online took the marketplace by surprise because businesses had thought that women, especially young women, would be reluctant to buy without first trying on the clothes. Because of this, many of the big Main Street retailers were slow to open online retail outlets, which gave an opportunity to sites like Asos. Aimed primarily at young adults, Asos had nearly five million registered users and thousands of products for sale, so the brand was an obvious partner for CRUK in its attempt to introduce a bit of commonsense thinking about skin protection.

A "Fashion Forecast" tool was developed on the Asos website in the summer of 2010, specifically for delivering CRUK's message. The tool was predominantly a personal style guide for users that allowed them to identify their own skin type using celebrity examples and to put in the occasion they were looking to buy a new outfit for and the likely weather. Users would get back a series of outfits that they could browse through and buy, along with fashion and skin protection advice.

Since most young women lap up this kind of fashion advice, adding skin protection advice to the routine of apparel choice made it not only palatable but fashionable. Asos promoted the Fashion Forecast tool to its entire user base through emails, newsletters, and Facebook. The campaign was further promoted in other places where the audience looked for celebrity-based fashion inspiration—celebrity gossip magazines *Heat* and *More*, and on Kiss FM radio.

A survey among the target audience showed that those who recalled the campaign were significantly more likely to have reported taking action to protect themselves from sunburn than those who didn't (80 percent versus 66 percent). Those who recalled the campaign were also significantly more likely than those who did not to report using a range of protective measures including using sunscreen, wearing a hat, and spending time in the shade.

No amount of telling this audience to dress sensibly would have made such a dramatic difference. Making the sun protection advice a part of their fashion choice helped to create a real change in attitude and made the truth palatable instead of unpleasant medicine. So a new routine—check the weather as well as check out what your favorite celebrity is up to—became the way of getting the truth across to a target market that had consistently avoided or ignored it.

No amount of telling this audience to dress sensibly would have made such a dramatic difference. Making the sun protection advice a part of their fashion choice helped to create a real change in attitude and made the truth palatable instead of unpleasant medicine.

Why did it work?

- **It is attached to an existing habit.** It's far easier to connect with an existing habit than it is to invent one from scratch, and it was a natural fit to add decision-relevant weather and skin protection information to making choices about outfits.

- **It added a helpful dimension to it versus distracting from it.** CRUK didn't sponsor the Fashion Forecast tool, but rather contributed to it. Sun protection became a quality of the deliverable, not just a helpful message (which would have likely been ignored).

- **It delivered behavior change.** In our view, by not calling out fear of sun damage as a decision that was individually actionable, the campaign made attending to it more likely as a quality of the overall experience. Awareness of the effects of the sun expanded the experience without drawing overt attention to its contribution.

Do as I Do, Not Just What I Say

One of the first things you learn as a parent is that parenting is a game of give and take. Much of what occurs is the result of compromise rather than your active choice or control; kids are the best negotiators in the world, so the best parental intentions are subject to change depending on circumstances. Parents have to constantly work to make what does happen at least somewhat resemble what should occur. These routines define family life, and it was recognizing one of these truths—that it's often tough to get kids to brush their teeth every night—that allowed Aquafresh not only to take some of the pain out of the archetypal battle of bedtime but also successfully sell its products.

In 2008, Aquafresh had developed three varieties to launch in the United Kingdom but had very little marketing budget to do so. Its "Milk Teeth" was aimed at kids under the age of three, its "Little Teeth" sub-brand was targeted for four- to six-year-olds, and its "Big Teeth" was for six- to nine-year-olds.

The traditional way to get mothers to buy one brand over another is to leverage guilt, all things considered. They're bombarded with imagery that suggests a kind of perfect housewifery and motherhood that in its extreme forms only exists in TV shows or movies from the 1950s. As a selling tool this can be remarkably effective, in part because the core components of responsible and authoritative parenting are not imaginary but rather a reasonable, noble goal. Advertising can often sensationalize these tendencies, as we're sure you can easily think of advertisements from not that long ago that sold by implying that if you don't buy this particular brand of household cleaner you're letting your family down, or even endangering them by exposure to bacteria and germs (remember what Purell chose *not* to do, as recounted earlier in this chapter).

So, it wasn't surprising that when Aquafresh's ad agency team at GlaxoSmithKline Consumer Healthcare spoke to moms, they uncovered a level of guilt about perfect motherhood that hasn't changed in a hundred years. Moms feel the same pressure now to be supermom as they did in the 1960s, when Betty Friedan wrote *The Feminine Mystique.* One of the focal points of their guilt was the dentist. Moms feel terrible if the regular dentist trip means that their kids need treatment, yet getting their kids to brush their teeth properly every night is often a point of conflict, so they end up feeling equally terrible about the routine and the outcome.

The bedtime battle proved to be evident in the blogosphere. One blogger, "Biz e-Mom," calculated that she'd spent "55 hours, 21 minutes, and 6 seconds" of her child's life wrestling with him at bedtime. Taking two hours a night for this task is just not sustainable, and she also said, "My son, Biz e-Baby2, is going for the MVP award or something on the opposing team, because that kid has been relentless." Her woes inspired research on possible solutions. Would a better-tasting toothpaste product shorten the battle time? A toothbrush that was somehow more fun? No, it wasn't that easy, according to the child care experts. The best solution was to create a bedtime ritual. And this insight proved to be the founding core of the Aquafresh brief. The team decided to help solve the dilemma by helping the bedtime teeth cleaning to occur.

The best solution was to create a bedtime ritual. And this insight proved to be the founding core of the Aquafresh brief.

To respect the insight, however, the team had to go beyond the obvious angles of trying to make the ritual fun. The Aquafresh team decided that it had to reflect the truth about the Battle of Bedtime that it had uncovered, and not present a glossy, perfect-world TV commercial that might be spot-on for the brand but fail to help moms successfully resolve their nightly challenges. Instead of showing some kind of fantasy advertisement of the aspirational perfect bedtime with a perfect mom helping her perfect kids clean their teeth before going to bed without complaint, the team took the brief to an absolute expert on the age group: Turner, owners of Cartoon Network and Cartoonito, the cartoon channel for preschool kids. The challenge: enable Aquafresh to get kids into a routine of brushing.

Turner created a ninety-second film to run on Cartoonito every night at bedtime (just before 7 p.m.) featuring "Nurdles," who were animated toothpaste characters who lead a group of real children singing and dancing along to a song entitled "Nurdle Schmurdle" that declared it was time to brush their teeth (and demonstrated how to do so properly). Designating a regular timeslot for the piece created a routine on which moms could rely, while giving them the ability to tune into a reminder for the family that it was time for teeth cleaning and for bed.

Watching the segment also allowed moms to avoid another kid routine—the "why" questions intended to prompt long, reasoned explanations that serve only to accomplish the delay in whatever action the kid is trying to avoid—and get out of the routine of having to declare angrily, "Because I told you so!" The Nurdles volunteered to take responsibility for this moment in the lives of moms and their kids, and did so in a way that was both entertaining and, by nature of its regularity, authoritative. If it's on TV, it must be true, right?

The campaign was extremely successful for the brand, and the role of the Nurdles has grown and grown. They're featured in magazine advertorials for kids, they have their own books, and they make appearances at the London Zoo and supermarkets around the United Kingdom. They have their own website, where you can play Nurdles video games, and the Nurdles song can be downloaded and played in the bathroom at whatever bedtime mom chooses.

Turner created genuinely lovable characters out of the Nurdles—Milky, Lilly, and Billy—and Aquafresh has gained huge market share by stepping outside of advertising spin and instead creating with them a helpful routine for moms with young kids.

If Aquafresh has stopped even just one tearful bedtime by creating a routine that's fun instead—and we think it's probably stopped thousands of tearful nights—then it is something to rejoice about. The core insight in this case is that the brand went beyond thinking about "choices" to understand the circumstances and routines in which its products are used. In doing it, the team discovered a truth about bedtimes that could also help it deliver a truth about its brand. Other solutions of this sort might not be as obvious, but we think that examining whether it is possible to create a ritual for a usage occasion delivers a truthful solution and a good commercial opportunity.

The core insight in this case is that the brand went beyond thinking about "choices" to understand the circumstances and routines in which its products are used.

FROM THE FORCES IN FAVOR OF ROT

It was 1950s America when moviegoers were introduced to a short film (called a "snipe") before the coming attraction trailers appeared. In it, four animated concession products—a pack of gum, bowl of popcorn, box of candy, and cup of soda—danced in a parade formation, singing, "Let's all go to the lobby" to the tune of "For He's a Jolly Good Fellow."

Loading up on concession food hadn't been a routine for moviegoers for most of history; in fact, while "fun" foods like popcorn were sold outside the early nickelodeon theaters, most operators didn't want the garbage and mess, hoping instead that patrons would associate the same upscale values to moviegoing that they did to live theater. It was only after World War II that the need for more revenue and the incipient threat of television moved owners to incorporate concession stands into their facilities and then encourage their use.

It worked. "Let's All Go to the Lobby" was so successful in helping teach a new generation of Americans a routine that in 2000 it was selected for preservation in the National Film Registry by the Library of Congress.

Conclusion

One of marketing's greatest adversaries is Clutter, the god of distraction who fills consumers' lives with activities and pursuits that keep them preoccupied and thus make them difficult to reach. He is a cruel and capricious being who dares us to push the limits of credulity and truth so that we may overcome him. We'll do just about anything to win that fight, sacrificing substance, utility, and sometimes truth (or a portion of it) so we can get that attention. We're so threatened by Clutter that many of our measures of success don't track the sales results we get from our marketing efforts but simply how effectively we're able to capture attention away from him. We work harder to earn the opportunity to say less. Clutter is the enemy who must be beaten at all costs, and it's a fight that gets harder with each new digital device, entertainment platform, TV channel, or other distraction he puts into the hands of consumers.

Clutter is the enemy who must be beaten at all costs, and it's a fight that gets harder with each new digital device, entertainment platform, TV channel, or other distraction he puts into the hands of consumers.

If we changed our perspective a bit, however, we might be able to see the challenge in a different way. Clutter is a top-down point of view. It's an aggregate picture of consumers engaged with and surrounded by a seemingly endless number of demands for their time and attention. Yet individually, those demands aren't distractions necessarily; they're the activities and habits of daily life. Some of them are quite enjoyable. Others are endured with little expenditure of emotion, and many are experienced almost unconsciously, by rote. Certainly a few are downright irritating. From a bottom-up point of view, while some of them are unique experiences, the vast majority of them are routines. Though it might seem like the way to combat Clutter is to try to invent exceptions to break his grasp, he gains his strength from these norms.

We say if you can't beat 'em, join 'em. Embracing the context of routines can be a very successful way to engage with consumers and, by doing so, communicate truth to them. At the risk of stretching the Clutter analogy too far, we'd say that perhaps the opportunity isn't so much to try to make your brand the solution to the problem of his reign and instead it is to figure out how to be part of the problem.

The idea of norms is very powerful, both as a descriptive framework for your content (as many of this chapter's examples illustrated), and as a contextual guide to the content itself. We spent less time on this second use because it's not easily applicable to the development of your marketing communications planning, but it's worth some of your thinking.

Routines aren't just "wrappers" for content but can also be a part of the content itself. Computer software is regularly updated. Magazine subscriptions deliver content and can be renewed automatically. Supplies of certain products can be replenished on a regular schedule. Many technology devices are always "on" so they can do things without our conscious command, or simply be ready to do them faster when we ask. Online forms are prepopulated with ordering information, website log-ins are saved, and many digital tools are customized to perform consistently in particular ways. Each of these contexts is in many ways synonymous with the content of the experiences. Our traditional marketing point of view takes them for granted somewhat, when they're really marketing vehicles and opportunities to communicate truth.

Applying these contextual qualities to your strategy is as easy as simply changing how you view the challenge and asking yourself, "Instead of trying to come up with ways to break routines, how can I strengthen and reinforce them?"

There are solid reasons why routines are an effective tool for delivering and expressing truth:

- **Known quantities.** A norm is known, both consciously and viscerally. There's no need to debate or prove any of its truths because they've already been created and delivered. This can be both for good and bad (it's why it's so hard for brands with bad histories to overcome consumer distrust), but working with it is required in either case. Why not correlate with known quantities instead of trying to invent new ones, or endeavoring to prove some known fact is different or wrong?

- **Allocated resources.** Consumers have already accounted for the time, cost, and energy required by their routines, so those variables don't have to be part of your pitch (unless you're improving them). "Givens" are called givens for a reason, and that's because they're already true. Again, this can be a positive or a negative, but either way, routines are established experiences, not new ideas.

- **Demonstrable outcomes.** People know the truth of their routines because they live them. Why focus your marketing strategy on changing or denying those truths when you could invent ways to reinforce them, literally using the context of proven routines to piggyback the delivering of your brand truths. References to "doing" are always going to be more powerful than asking consumers for "thinking" time.

If you're at all like us, you'd be happy not to do battle with Clutter at every turn. Exceptions are desperately hard to deliver, as Clutter's distractions make it so hard to overcome. The truth that routines prove is what contributes to the sometimes high barriers to entry of habits, and it's why people tend to revert to what they already do and know. Routines are far easier to encourage than to break. While award-winning branding campaigns might be exceptional, successful selling is the norm for great brands.

ROUTINE CHECKLIST

1. What are the regular routines of your consumers? Into which of them does your product or service fit?

2. Can you create a new routine for them that belongs to your brand or change an old one to become exclusively yours?

3. Can you revive a traditional, fondly remembered routine in order to grab a greater share of your consumers' attention?

4. Is there a habit you can leverage? Something that you wouldn't automatically attach to your brand but can make great sense?

5. What rewards can you give the consumer for adopting a new routine (hint: think tangible, not emotional)?

6. What could you give them to encourage them to maintain a routine instead of reconsidering its utility?

7. Are there things that you can take off the table of your consumers' awareness (or required actions) in order to simplify their lives? Could you position these deliverables as truths about your brand?

8. If there is an update, renewal, or replacement built into the experience of your product or service, could you make such instances utterly seamless and routine?

9. Is your main competitor another brand in your category or simply the idea that your customer could at any time change his or her mind? If you identify the risk as the latter, how might you reconsider your brand truths to address such risks instead of the competitive set?

10. If your next marketing plan had to be centered on an operational improvement to your offering, what would it be?

Epilogue

And Finally, What's Next?

This book is a manifesto for your brand to tell the truth. We knew our position on the subject when we started out to write it, but in doing so we only became more convinced that truth is the emerging way to think about your brand and marketing. Everything else pales in comparison: advertising spin is redundant; conversation without purpose is purposeless, no matter how funny; meaning isn't something your brand can buy when marketers decide to give to a charity or otherwise skip talking about selling stuff. These are all behaviors and, as such, they communicate truths about your brand. Such behaviors are, by definition, at odds with brand images that most brands creatively and selectively choose to publicly present. Promoting a brand image that is at odds with the truth of behaviors means wasting every dollar or pound spent, or at least not getting your full value. Your consumers aren't getting value for their money, either.

It's better to spend money training your employees to be warm and helpful than on any amount of advertising claiming brand warmth. The metrics of advertising image and recall are irrelevant when the thing that you'll be remembered for most is how short the experience you promised comes up against expectations, how long it takes you to apologize for something gone wrong, or how distant your marketing content was from the actual wants and needs of your customers. It's better to use conversation to establish and maintain better understanding of the truth with your various stakeholder audiences.

The metrics of advertising image and recall are irrelevant when the thing that you'll be remembered for most is how short the experience you promised comes up against expectations, how long it takes you to apologize for something gone wrong, or how distant your marketing content was from the actual wants and needs of your customers.

It is no good denying this fact. It is no good bemoaning it. It is time to face it. The good news is that drawing on a century or so of becoming an expert at selling the sizzle, not the steak, your competitors are probably behind where you are right now because you've just read this manual about brand truth and how to deliver it. You've seen through our numerous examples that truth really does sell.

Truth sells in a world where consumers are the experts who know everything about you. They are the experts to whom other consumers turn for advice about you. What they don't know already they can find out in thirty seconds on their smartphone. (This isn't as snappy as Ogilvy's original statement, we know.) You can't spin the facts to consumers or distract them entertainingly like you used to. If you think you can, we want you to consider trying these brand truth techniques instead.

Truth sells for an advertising and marketing industry that is tiring of relying on the latest-and-greatest tricks to renew outdated models for reaching consumers. Our marketing needs a truly new way of working. Creative work can't be developed in contradiction to the truth that everyone really thinks about any and every advertised product and service. No media strategy (paid or earned) is doing enough if it just sticks ads or content in front of the target consumer. It needs to work to ensure that the truth communicated is delivered in the most cogent and convincing way.

We've reviewed some great examples of marketing strategy in these pages that illustrate how brand truth isn't just unavoidable but preferable. Brand truth is additive, too; get it right, and the consumer will feel the pull of your marketing like iron filings are pulled to the magnetic north.

The techniques we've covered are essentials in an effective strategy in the age of dialogue:

- Acknowledge reality; don't put lipstick on a pig.
- Deliver services or activities that make your brand truth real to people.
- Take the consumer on your brand truth journey with you.
- Enlist others in expressing truths. (If a third party says it, then it is twice as convincing.)
- Get physically up close and personal by really being local—ideally very local and specific.
- Create moments that are undeniable by using the power of Truth Turning Points.
- Use point-of-action media.

- Address contexts when your communications have most meaning.
- Establish routines and making new rituals around your brand that make clutter an ally, not an enemy.

The good news is that a commitment to brand truth doesn't mean being somber and serious all the time. The case studies in these pages show humor being successful at truth-telling, surprises working really well, and warmth and closeness helping to deliver great outcomes. It also doesn't mean that you have to stop communicating what you think about the brand and just rely on user-generated content and the so-called wisdom of the crowd. You can and should still broadcast your own brand image truth. Just be prepared to be open to the consumer and to share the truth with them.

Many of the metrics around perception and likability that have supported the old age of marketing are anachronistic, and they don't capture the true power of our least new media tools. There are many shibboleths that need destroying in this arena. For instance, allowing that PR activity (online or off) is not really accountable is nonsense. So is only justifying return on investment by measuring the meaning delivered by advertising gross rating points to consumers' claimed behavior. Just as we need new ways of making marketing strategies real, we also need new standards of measuring their success.

We're very optimistic about the opportunities truth presents for brands, their agencies, and consumers. The truth is, after all, undeniable. Some marketing strategies need a wake-up call. You only have to turn on the TV or glance at a billboard to see the content that some of your competitors think they can get away with, or have been persuaded to run by the architects of spin. However, brand truth strategies are more visible, too. More and more marketers are turning away from easily constructed spin and digging deep into the truth of their brands. We believe that in five years we'll look back on the art of spin as an anachronism.

More and more marketers are turning away from easily constructed spin and digging deep into the truth of their brands. We believe that in five years we'll look back on the art of spin as an anachronism.

The truth is the true future of successful marketing.

We're truly grateful that you gave our ideas a chance. Please let us know what you're doing and thinking at our *Tell the Truth* website: www.tellthetruthbook.com.

About the Authors

Sue Unerman is Chief Strategy Officer at MediaCom and has experience in planning and buying media at Benton & Bowles, DMB&B, and Geers Gross Advertising. *Campaign* magazine says Unerman is "widely considered to be one of media's finest strategic brains." She lives in London. She blogs at http://sueunerman.com/.

Sue dedicates this book to Mark, Sylvia, and Georgia.

Jonathan Salem Baskin is president of Baskin Associates, Inc., a marketing decisions consultancy. He has worked on branding strategy for global brand names, including Apple, Blockbuster, and Nissan. He writes a column on marketing leadership for *Advertising Age* and blogs at *Histories of Social Media* and *Dim Bulb*. He lives in Chicago. You can learn more about Jonathan at http://baskinbrand.com.

Index